P.L.S.B.,
Hereford,
14.3.78

# Prayers of the Eucharist:
## Early and Reformed

# Prayers of the Eucharist: Early and Reformed

Texts translated and edited by

R. C. D. JASPER AND
G. J. CUMING

COLLINS

Collins Publishers
Liturgical Publications, 187 Piccadilly, London, w.1

First published 1975
ISBN 0 00 599529 9

Set in Monotype Bembo
Made and printed in Great Britain by
Wm Collins Sons & Co Ltd, Glasgow

# Contents

# Preface

There is a widespread tendency for liturgical texts to go out of print.
To meet this deficiency we here present texts in English of thirty-six
eucharistic services or descriptions of services from early times until
1662. This date has been chosen as the *terminus ad quem* because later
rites are still available in other collections. Our chief object has been to
indicate how each rite handles the four main actions of the eucharist:
taking, giving thanks, breaking and giving. The rest of each rite has
been set out in skeleton form. Two anaphoras – those of Saints Addai
and Mari and of Basil of Caesarea – are printed without the skeleton for
the sake of the very early elements which they contain: the other
elements of these services are of much later date.

All translations are our own, except where otherwise specified. We
have used 'you' rather than 'thou', except in texts actually written in a
'thou' form in English; and in these the spelling and punctuation have
been modernized. The translations aim at literal exactitude rather than
elegance.

The bibliographies are patently not exhaustive, but seek only to
indicate where the original text may be found, and to list books and
articles that are relatively easily accessible to the English-speaking
student. Failing these, we have included a few titles in French. References are given wherever possible to the following collections of
texts:

F. E. Brightman, *Liturgies Eastern and Western* (1896, reprinted 1965)
– quoted as *L.E.W.*

A. Hänggi and I. Pahl, *Prex Eucharistica* (1968) – quoted as *Prex
Eucharistica*.

Bard Thompson, *Liturgies of the Western Church* (1961) – quoted as
Bard Thompson.

Other frequently-cited works are:

> G. Dix, *The Shape of the Liturgy* (1945) – quoted as Dix, *The Shape*.
> L. Bouyer, *Eucharist* (1970 – translation of *Eucharistie*, 1966) – quoted as Bouyer.
> G. J. Cuming, *The Anglican Liturgy* (1969) – quoted as Cuming.

We are grateful for permission to reproduce the following copyright texts: ch. 32, John Knox: *The Forme of Prayers and Ministration of the Sacraments* 1556, from W. D. Maxwell, *The Liturgical Portions of the Geneva Service Book*, Faith Press, 1965; ch. 36, extracts from the *Book of Common Prayer* 1662, Crown Copyright.

A great many of the texts we have used may be found in A. Hamman and T. Halton, *The Mass* (1967): but unfortunately this collection was not available to us during our work on this book. Every effort has been made to utilize the oldest and most reliable sources, including some which have come to light only in the last ten years or so.

*January* 1975                                    R. C. D. JASPER
                                                  G. J. CUMING

# I

# Jewish Prayers

## Blessing for Food (*Birkath Hammazon*)

The *Birkath hammazon* is a thanksgiving after a meal, and is thought by scholars to be a possible ultimate source of the Christian eucharistic thanksgiving, especially in view of its use in the Passover meal. While most of the blessing is at least contemporary with the lifetime of Jesus, the fourth section was added only after the fall of Jerusalem in A.D. 70.

The text translated below is that of the *Siddur Rav Saadya*, from a tenth-century manuscript.

**BIBLIOGRAPHY**
*Prex Eucharistica*, pp. 10–12.
L. Finkelstein, 'The birkat ha-mazon', in *The Jewish Quarterly Review*, 19 (1928–9), pp. 211–62.
Dix, *The Shape*, pp. 50–6, 214–25.
Bouyer, pp. 50–90.
L. Ligier, (1) 'From the Last Supper to the Eucharist', in L. C. Sheppard (ed.), *The New Liturgy* (1970), pp. 113–50.
(2) 'The Origins of the Eucharistic Prayer', in *Studia Liturgica*, 9 (1973), pp. 161–85.

*Blessing of him who nourishes*
Blessed are you, Lord our God, King of the universe, for you nourish us and the whole world with goodness, grace, kindness and mercy.
Blessed are you, Lord, for you nourish the universe.

*Blessing for the earth*
We will give thanks to you, Lord our God, because you have given us for our inheritance a desirable land, good and wide, the covenant and the law, life and food.
(*On the feasts of* Hanukkah *and* Purim, *here follows an embolism*.)

9

And for all these things we give you thanks and bless your name for ever and beyond.

Blessed are you, Lord our God, for the earth and for food.

*Blessing for Jerusalem*

Have mercy, Lord our God, on us your people Israel, and your city Jerusalem, on your sanctuary and your dwelling-place, on Zion, the habitation of your glory, and the great and holy house over which your name is invoked. Restore the kingdom of the house of David to its place in our days, and speedily build Jerusalem.

(*On the feast of* Passover, *here follows this embolism:*

Our God and God of our fathers, may there arise in your sight, and come, and be present, and be regarded, and be pleasing, and be heard, and be visited, and be remembered our remembrance and our visitation, and the remembrance of our fathers, and the remembrance of the Messiah, the son of your servant David, and the remembrance of Jerusalem, the city of your holiness, and the remembrance of all your people, the house of Israel: for escape, for prosperity, for grace, and for loving-kindness and mercy, for life and for peace, on this day of the Feast of Unleavened Bread. Remember us on this day, Lord our God, for prosperity, and visit us on it for blessing, and save us on it for life. And by the word of salvation and mercy spare us, and grant us grace, and have mercy on us, and save us: for our eyes look to you, for you, O God, are a gracious and merciful king.

Blessed are you, Lord, for you build Jerusalem. Amen.)

*Blessing of the good and beneficent*

Blessed are you, Lord our God, King of the universe, God, our father, our king, our creator, our redeemer, good and beneficent king, who day by day is concerned to benefit us in many ways, and himself will increase us for ever in grace and kindness and spirit and mercy and every good thing.

# 2

# The New Testament

The New Testament accounts of the Last Supper reflect two different traditions, one in Mark and Matthew, the other in 1 Corinthians and Luke. In addition, there are accounts in the Gospels of Jesus breaking bread before and after the Last Supper; and elsewhere in the New Testament the eucharist is entitled 'the breaking of bread'. The Greek word '*anamnēsis*', here translated 'remembrance', has no exact equivalent in English.

BIBLIOGRAPHY
J. Jeremias, *The Eucharistic Words of Jesus* (1966).
See also bibliography for *Jewish Prayers*, p. 9 above.
*The Revised Standard Version Common Bible* (1973).

*Mark 6.41* Taking the five loaves and the two fish, (Jesus) looked up to heaven, and blessed, and broke the loaves, and gave them to the disciples to set before the people; and he divided the two fish among them all.
= *Matthew 14.18; Luke 9.16.*
*Cf. Mark 8.6–7; Matthew 15.36; John 6.11.*

| *Mark 14.22–25* | *Matthew 26.26–29* |
|---|---|
| 22 And as they were eating, he took bread, and blessed, and broke it, and gave it to them, and said, 'Take; this is my body.' 23 And he took a cup, and when he had given thanks he gave it to them, and they all drank of it. 24 And he said to them, 'This is my blood of the covenant, which is poured out for many. 25 Truly, I say to you, I shall not drink | 26 Now as they were eating, *Jesus* took bread, and blessed, and broke it, and gave it to the *disciples* and said, 'Take, *eat*; this is my body.' 27 And he took a cup, and when he had given thanks he gave it to them, *saying*, 'Drink of it, all *of you*; 28 *for* this is my blood of the covenant, which is poured out for many *for the forgiveness of sins*. 29 I tell you I shall not drink again |

again of the fruit of the vine until that day when I drink it new in the kingdom of God.'

of *this* fruit of the vine until that day when I drink it new *with you* in *my Father's kingdom.*'

### Luke 22.15–20

15 And he said to them, 'I have earnestly desired to eat this passover with you before I suffer; 16 for I tell you I shall not eat it until it is fulfilled in the kingdom of God.' 17 And he took a cup, and when he had given thanks he said, 'Take this, *and divide it among yourselves*; 18 for I tell you that from now on I shall not drink of the fruit of the vine until the kingdom of God *comes*.' 19 And he took bread, and when he had given thanks he broke it *and gave it to them*, saying, 'This is my body which is *given* for you. Do this in remembrance of me.' 20 And likewise the cup after supper, saying, 'This cup *which is poured out for you* is the new covenant in my blood.'

### 1 Corinthians 11.23–26

23 For I received from the Lord what I also delivered to you, that the Lord Jesus on the night when he was betrayed took bread, 24 and when he had given thanks, he broke it, and said, 'This is my body which is for you. Do this in remembrance of me.' 25 In the same way also the cup, after supper, saying, 'This is the new covenant in my blood. Do this, as often as you drink it, in remembrance of me.' 26 For as often as you eat this bread and drink the cup, you proclaim the Lord's death until he comes.

*Luke 24.30, 35*   30 When he was at the table with them, he took the bread and blessed, and broke it, and gave it to them . . . 35 Then they told . . . how he was known to them in the breaking of the bread. (*Cf. John 21.13.*)

*Acts 2.42, 46, 47*   42 And they devoted themselves to the apostles' teaching and fellowship, to the breaking of bread and the prayers . . . 46 And day by day, attending the temple together and breaking bread in their homes, they partook of food with glad and generous hearts, 47 praising God and having favour with all the people.

*Acts 20.7, 11*   7 On the first day of the week, when we were gathered together to break bread, Paul talked with them . . . 11 And when Paul had gone up and had broken bread and eaten, he conversed with them a long while, until daybreak .   .

*Acts 27.35*   And when he had said this, he took bread, and giving thanks to God in the presence of all he broke it and began to eat.

*1 Corinthians 10.16*   The cup of blessing which we bless, is it not a participation in the blood of Christ? The bread which we break, is it not a participation in the body of Christ?

# 3

# The *Didache*

*The Teaching of the Twelve Apostles*, commonly known as the *Didache*, was rediscovered in 1873. When and where it was written is unknown, and widely differing answers have been given to both questions. It has been allotted dates varying from A.D. 60 to the third century; and both Egypt and Syria have been suggested as its country of origin. It also remains open to argument whether the prayers it contains belong to an *agape*, a eucharist, or to two separate services. The work was written in Greek; a Coptic version has some interesting variant readings.

BIBLIOGRAPHY
*Prex Eucharistica*, pp. 66–8.
F. E. Vokes, *The Riddle of the Didache* (1938).
    'The Didache still debated', in *Church Quarterly*, 3 (1970), pp. 57–62.
J. P. Audet, *La Didaché: Instruction des Apôtres* (1958).
Bouyer, pp. 115–19.

CHAPTERS 1–6: 'THE TWO WAYS'
CHAPTER 7: BAPTISM
CHAPTER 8: FASTING

CHAPTER 9
  1  *About the thanksgiving: give thanks thus:*
  2  *First, about the cup:*
  We give thanks to you, our Father, for the holy vine of your child[1] David, which you made known to us through your child[1] Jesus; glory to you for evermore.
  3  *And about the broken bread:*
  We give thanks to you, our Father, for the life and knowledge

  1. Or servant; *cf. Acts 3.13, etc.*

14

which you made known to us through your child[2] Jesus; glory to you for evermore.

4  As this broken bread was scattered over the mountains and when brought together became one, so let your Church be brought together from the ends of the earth into your kingdom; for yours are the glory and the power [3]through Jesus Christ[3] for evermore.

5  *But let no one eat or drink of your eucharist but those who have been baptized in the name of the Lord. For about this also the Lord has said, 'Do not give what is holy to the dogs.'*

## CHAPTER 10

1  *And after you have had your fill, give thanks thus:*

2  We give thanks to you, holy Father, for your holy name which you have enshrined in our hearts, and for the knowledge and faith and immortality which you made known to us through your child[2] Jesus; glory to you for evermore.

3  You, Lord Almighty, created all things for the sake of your name and gave food and drink to men for their enjoyment, that they might give you thanks; but to us you have granted spiritual food and drink for eternal life through your child[2] Jesus.

4  Above all we give you thanks because you are mighty; glory to you for evermore. Amen.

5  Remember, Lord, your Church, to deliver it from all evil and to perfect it in your love, and bring it together from the four winds, [4]now sanctified,[4] into your kingdom which you have prepared for it; for yours are the power and the glory for evermore. Amen.

6  May grace[5] come, and this world pass away. Amen.
Hosanna to the God[6] of David.
If any be holy, let him come; if any be not, let him repent.
*Marana tha.* Amen.

7  *But allow the prophets to give thanks as much as they wish.*

---

2. Or servant; *cf. Acts 3.13, etc.*  
4. *Coptic omits.*  
6. *Coptic:* house.  

3. *Coptic omits.*  
5. *Coptic:* the Lord.

CHAPTERS 11–13: PROPHETS

CHAPTER 14

1  *On the Lord's day of the Lord, come together, break bread, and give thanks, having first confessed your transgressions, that your sacrifice may be pure.*

2  *But let none who has a quarrel with his companion join with you until they have been reconciled, that your sacrifice may not be defiled.*

3  *For this is that which was spoken by the Lord, 'In every place and at every time offer me a pure sacrifice; for I am a great king, says the Lord, and my name is wonderful among the nations.'*

CHAPTER 15: CHURCH DISCIPLINE
CHAPTER 16: THE LAST DAY

# 4

## Justin Martyr

Justin was born in Syria, and was converted to Christianity c. A.D. 130. His *Dialogue with Trypho* (a Jew) was written at Ephesus c. 135. Justin later went to Rome, where he wrote the *First Apology* c. 150. This includes an outline of the eucharist, the earliest that has survived. Justin describes it in two contexts: first, following a baptism; secondly, as the ordinary Sunday service.

BIBLIOGRAPHY
*Prex Eucharistica*, pp. 68–74.
L. W. Barnard, *Justin Martyr, His Life and Thought* (1967), ch. x, esp. pp. 142–50.
Dix, *The Shape*, pp. 222–4.
J. A. Jungmann, *The Early Liturgy* (1960), pp. 40–4.

## Dialogue with Trypho

41.1 The offering of fine flour . . . which was handed down to be offered by those who were cleansed from leprosy, was a type of the bread of the eucharist, which our Lord Jesus Christ handed down to us to do for the remembrance of the suffering which he suffered for those who are cleansed in their souls from all wickedness of men, so that we might give thanks to God, both for creating the world with all things that are in it for the sake of man, and for freeing us from the evil in which we were born, and for accomplishing a complete destruction of the principalities and powers through him who suffered according to his will.

2 Hence God speaks about the sacrifices which were then offered by you, as I said before, through Malachi, one of the twelve (prophets):

My will is not in you, says the Lord, and I will not receive your sacrifices from your hands; for, from the rising of the sun to its setting, my name has been glorified among the nations, and in every place incense is offered to my name and a pure sacrifice, for my name is great among the nations, says the Lord, but you profane it.

3   He is prophesying about the sacrifices which are offered in every place by us, the nations, that is the bread of the eucharist and likewise the cup of the eucharist, saying that we glorify his name, but you profane it . . .

117.1   So God bears witness in advance that he is well pleased with all the sacrifices in his name, which Jesus the Christ handed down to be done, namely in the eucharist of the bread and the cup, which are done in every place of the world by the Christians.

2   . . . Now I myself also say that prayers and thanksgivings made by worthy men are the only sacrifices that are perfect and well-pleasing to God.

3   For these alone have been handed down for Christians to do, even in the remembrance of their solid and liquid food, in which also they remember the suffering which the Son of God suffered for them.

## First Apology

65.1   After we have thus baptized him who has believed and has given his assent, we take him to those who are called brethren where they are assembled, to make common prayers earnestly for ourselves and for him who has been enlightened[1] and for all others everywhere, that, having learned the truth, we may be deemed worthy to be found good citizens in our actions and guardians of the commandments, so that we may be saved with eternal salvation.

2   When we have ended the prayers, we greet one another with a kiss.

3   Then bread and a cup of water and of mixed wine[2] are brought to him who presides over the brethren, and he takes them and offers praise and glory to the Father of all in the name of the Son and of the Holy Spirit, and gives thanks at some length that we have been deemed worthy of these things from him. When he has finished the prayers and the thanksgiving, all the people present give their assent by saying, 'Amen.'

---

1. *i.e., by baptism.*        2. *It is not clear whether Justin means one cup or two cups.*

4  Amen is Hebrew for 'So be it'.

5  And when the president has given thanks and all the people have assented, those whom we call deacons give to each one present a portion of the bread and wine and water over which thanks have been given,[3] and take them to those who are not present.

66.1  And we call this food 'thanksgiving';[4] and no one may partake of it unless he is convinced of the truth of our teaching, and has been cleansed with the washing for forgiveness of sins and regeneration, and lives as Christ handed down.

2  For we do not receive these things as common bread or common drink; but just as our Saviour Jesus Christ, being incarnate through the word of God, took flesh and blood for our salvation, so too we have been taught that the food over which thanks have been given [5]by the prayer of the Word who is from him,[5] from which our flesh and blood are fed by transformation, is both the flesh and blood of that incarnate Jesus.

3  For the apostles in the records composed by them which are called gospels, have handed down what was commanded them: that Jesus took bread, gave thanks, and said, 'Do this for my remembrance; this is my body'; and likewise he took the cup, gave thanks, and said, 'This is my blood'; and gave to them alone.

4  And the evil demons have imitated this and ordered it to be done also in the mysteries of Mithras. For as you know or may learn, bread and a cup of water are used with certain formulas in their rites of initiation.

67.1  And thereafter we continually remind one another of these things. Those who have the means help all those in need; and we are always together.

2  And we bless the Maker of all things through his Son Jesus Christ and through the Holy Spirit over all that we receive.

3  And on the day called Sun-day an assembly is held in one place of all who live in town or country, and the records of the apostles or writings of the prophets are read for as long as time allows.

3. Greek: *eucharistēthentos*.        4. Greek: *eucharistia*.
5. Or by a word of prayer that is from him *or* by a prayer of the word that is from him.

4   Then, when the reader has finished, the president in a discourse admonishes and exhorts (us) to imitate these good things.

5   Then we all stand up together and offer prayers; and as we said before, when we have finished praying, bread and wine and water are brought up, and the president likewise offers prayers and thanksgivings to the best of his ability, and the people assent, saying the Amen; and there is a distribution, and everyone participates in (the elements) over which thanks have been given; and they are sent through the deacons to those who are not present.

6   And the wealthy who so desire give what they wish, as each chooses; and what is collected is deposited with the president.

7   He helps orphans and widows, and those who through sickness or any other cause are in need, and those in prison, and strangers sojourning among us; in a word, he takes care of all those who are in need.

8   And we all assemble together on Sun-day, because it is the first day, on which God, having transformed the darkness and matter, made the world; and Jesus Christ our Saviour rose from the dead the same day; for they crucified him the day before Saturday; and the day after Saturday, which is Sun-day, he appeared to his apostles and disciples, and taught them these things which we have presented to you for your consideration.

# 5

# Hippolytus: *The Apostolic Tradition*

*The Apostolic Tradition* of Hippolytus is generally believed to have survived in the form of an anonymous, untitled work which in the nineteenth century was given the name of *The Egyptian Church Order*. This has come down to us in Latin, Coptic, Arabic, and Ethiopic versions, and in various adaptations such as *The Apostolic Constitutions* (see pp. 65-74) and the *Testamentum Domini*. Its identification with the work of Hippolytus was proposed by E. Schwartz (1910) and R. H. Connolly (1916), and implies a date of *c.* A.D. 215. The work professedly reflects 'the tradition which has remained until now', and so may be taken as a witness to Roman practice some fifty years earlier. This brings it close to the time of Justin, with whose account it agrees quite closely. Like Justin, Hippolytus describes two eucharists, one following the consecration of a bishop, the other after a baptism. He gives us the earliest surviving text of a eucharistic prayer, but this should be regarded as an individual specimen rather than as an invariable form.

Since the original Greek is largely lost, the translation is necessarily debatable. Here chapters 4, 5, 6, 22 and 23 (Dix's numbering; in Botte's they are 4, 5, 6 and 21) are translated from the Latin; chapter 10 (Botte 9), which is lacking from the Latin, from the Sahidic Coptic version.

BIBLIOGRAPHY

B. Botte, *La Tradition Apostolique de Saint Hippolyte* (1972).
G. Dix, *The Apostolic Tradition of Saint Hippolytus* (1968, ed. H. Chadwick).
R. H. Connolly, 'The Eucharistic Prayer of Hippolytus', in *Journal of Theological Studies*, 39 (1938), pp. 350-69.
G. Dix, *The Shape*, pp. 157-62.
J. A. Jungmann, *The Early Liturgy* (1960), pp. 52-73.
Bouyer, pp. 158-82.

CHAPTER 1: PROLOGUE
CHAPTERS 2, 3: CONSECRATION OF A BISHOP

CHAPTER 4: THE EUCHARIST

1   *And when he has been made bishop, all shall offer the kiss of peace, greeting him because[1] he has been made worthy.*

2   *Then the deacons shall present the offering to him; and he, laying his hands on it with all the presbytery, shall say, giving thanks:*

3   The Lord be with you.[2]

*And all shall say:*

> And with your spirit.
>
> Up with your hearts.[3]
>
> We have them with the Lord.
>
> Let us give thanks to the Lord.
>
> It is fitting and right.

*And then he shall continue thus:*

4   We render thanks to you, O God, through your beloved child[4] Jesus Christ, whom in the last times you sent to us as saviour and redeemer and angel of your will;

5   who is your inseparable Word, through whom you made all things, and in whom you were well pleased.

6   You sent him from heaven into the Virgin's womb; and, conceived in the womb, he was made flesh and was manifested as your Son, being born of the Holy Spirit and the Virgin.

7   Fulfilling your will and gaining for you a holy people, he stretched out his hands when he should suffer, that he might release from suffering those who have believed in you.

8   And when he was betrayed to voluntary suffering that he might destroy death, and break the bonds of the devil, and tread down hell, and shine upon the righteous, and fix the limit, and manifest the resurrection,

9   he took bread and gave thanks to you, saying, 'Take, eat; this is my body, which shall be broken for you.' Likewise also the cup, saying, 'This is my blood, which is shed for you;

10   when you do this, you make my remembrance.'

---

1. *Or that.*     2. Coptic *adds* all.     3. *The Latin has no verb.*
4. *Or servant (cf.* Didache, *p.* 14).

11  Remembering therefore his death and resurrection, we offer to you the bread and the cup, giving you thanks because you have held us worthy to stand before you and minister to you.

12  And we ask that you would send your Holy Spirit upon the offering of your holy Church; that, gathering them into one, you would grant to all who partake of the holy things (to partake) for the fullness of the Holy Spirit for the confirmation of faith in truth;[5]

13  that we may praise and glorify you through your child[6] Jesus Christ, through whom be glory and honour to you, to the Father and the Son with the Holy Spirit, in your holy Church, both now and to the ages of ages. (Amen.)

### CHAPTER 5: THE BLESSING OF OIL

1  *If anyone offers oil, (the bishop) shall render thanks in the same way as for the offering of bread and wine, not saying (it) word for word but with similar effect, saying:*

2  O God, sanctifier of this oil, as you [7]give health to[7] those who use[8] and receive (that) with which you anointed kings, priests, and prophets, so may it give strength to all those who taste it and health to all that use it.

### CHAPTER 6: THE BLESSING OF CHEESE AND OLIVES

1  *Likewise if anyone offers cheese and olives, he shall say thus:*

2  Sanctify this milk which has been coagulated, coagulating us also to your love.

3  Make this fruit of the olive not to depart from your sweetness, which is an example of your richness which you have poured from the tree of life to them that hope in you.

4  *But in every blessing shall be said:*

To you be glory, to the Father and the Son with the Holy Spirit, in the holy Church, both now and always and to all the ages of ages. (Amen.)

---

5.  *The Latin is almost untranslatable at this point. Literally translated,* 'grant' *has no object; hence the addition of* 'to partake'. *Testamentum Domini reads:* 'Grant to all who partake of the holy things to be united with you for filling with Holy Spirit for the confirmation of faith in truth'; *this may be closer to the original.*

6.  Cf. note 4.        7.  *Dix conjectures:* sanctify.

8.  Ethiopic: are anointed (*which Dix and Botte prefer*).

CHAPTER 7: SPURIOUS PRAYERS

CHAPTERS 8.1–10.2: PRIESTS, DEACONS AND CONFESSORS

CHAPTER 10

3   *And the bishop shall give thanks according to what we said above.*

4   *It is not at all necessary for him to say the same words as we said above, as though trying (to say them) from memory, when giving thanks to God; but let each pray according to his ability.*

5   *If indeed he is able to pray sufficiently long with a solemn prayer, it is good. But if, when he prays, he recites a prayer according to a fixed form, no one shall prevent him. Only, let his prayer be correct and orthodox.*

CHAPTERS 11–15: MINOR ORDERS

CHAPTERS 16–19: CATECHUMENS

CHAPTERS 20, 21: BAPTISM

CHAPTER 22

1   *Post-baptismal prayer.*

2   *Anointing.*

3, 4   *Sealing.*

5   *Thenceforward (the newly-baptized) shall pray together with all the people; but they shall not previously pray with the faithful unless they have carried out all these things.*

6   *And after the prayers, let them offer the kiss of peace.*

CHAPTER 23: THE PASCHAL EUCHARIST

1   *And then let the offering be brought up by the deacons to the bishop: and he shall give thanks over the bread for the representation, which the Greeks call antitype, of the body of Christ; and the cup mixed with wine* [9]*for the antitype, which the Greeks call likeness* [9], *of the blood which was shed for all who have believed in him;*

2   *(and over) milk and honey mixed together in fulfilment of the promise which was made to (our) fathers, in which he said, 'a land flowing with milk and honey'; in which also Christ gave his flesh, through which those who believe are nourished like little children, making the bitterness of the heart*

9. *Botte conjectures:* for the likeness, which the Greeks call *homoiōma.*

*sweet by the gentleness of his word;*

3    *and (over) water, as an offering to signify the washing, that the inner man also, which is the soul, may receive the same things as the body.*

4    *And the bishop shall give a reason for all these things to those who receive.*

5    *And when he breaks the bread, in distributing fragments to each, he shall say:*

The bread of heaven in Christ Jesus.

6    *And he who receives shall answer:* Amen.

7    *And if there are not enough presbyters, the deacons also shall hold the cups, and stand by in good order and reverence: first, he who holds the water; second, the milk; third, the wine.*

8    *And they who receive* [10]*shall taste of each thrice, he who gives it saying*[10]: In God the Father Almighty.
*And he who receives shall say:* Amen.

9    And in the Lord Jesus Christ. (Amen.)

10    And in the holy Spirit and the holy Church.
*And he shall say:* Amen.

11    *So shall it be done to each one.*

## CHAPTERS 24–38: OTHER CHURCH OBSERVANCES

---

10. Or shall taste of each, he who gives it saying thrice.

# 6

# The Anaphora of
# Saints Addai and Mari

This liturgy originated in Edessa, a city of north-eastern Syria near the frontier between the Roman Empire and Persia, and one of the earliest centres of Christianity. After the Council of Ephesus (A.D. 431) the area became Nestorian, and was subsequently occupied by the Arabs. These two circumstances kept the liturgy relatively free from Byzantine influence; and though in a developed form it is still in use today, it is likely that its oldest parts go back to the third century. The oldest known manuscript lacks the priest's private prayers found in later copies, and the Sanctus is generally thought to be an interpolation. Scholars are divided about the apparent absence of an institution narrative and the authenticity of the epiclesis.

The text translated below is that recently found in the Church of Mar Esha'ya, Mosul, which was written in the eleventh or twelfth century. The congregational parts are completed below from other early manuscripts.

BIBLIOGRAPHY

W. F. Macomber, 'The oldest known text of the Anaphora of the Apostles Addai and Mari', in *Orientalia Christiana Periodica*, 32 (1966), pp. 335–71.

E. J. Cutrone, 'The Anaphora of the Apostles: Implications of the Mar Eša'ya Text', in *Theological Studies*, 34 (1973), pp. 624–42.

Dix, *The Shape*, pp. 178–87.

Bouyer, pp. 146–58.

*Priest:*   Peace be with you.
*Answer:*   And with you and your spirit.
*Priest:*   The grace of our Lord (Jesus Christ and the love of God the Father, and the fellowship of the Holy Spirit be with us all now and ever world without end).
*Answer:*   Amen.

*Priest:*   Up with your minds.

*Answer:*   They are with you, O God.

*Priest:*   The offering is offered to God, the Lord of all.

*Answer:*   It is fitting and right.

*The priest says privately:* Worthy of glory from every mouth and thanksgiving from every tongue is the adorable and glorious name of the Father and of the Son and of the Holy Spirit. He created the world through his grace and its inhabitants through his kindness; he saved men through his mercy, and gave great grace to mortals. Your majesty, O Lord, a thousand thousand heavenly beings adore, myriad myriads of angels, and ranks of spiritual beings, ministers of fire and spirit, together with the holy cherubim and seraphim, glorify your name, crying out and glorifying (unceasingly calling to one another and saying:)

*People:* Holy, holy, (holy, Lord God Almighty; heaven and earth are full of his praises).

*The priest says privately:* And with these heavenly armies, Lord, we also, your lowly, weak and miserable servants give you thanks because you have brought about in us a great grace which cannot be repaid. For you put on our human nature to give us life through your divine nature; you raised us from our lowly state; you restored our fall; you restored our immortality; you forgave our debts; you justified our sinfulness; you enlightened our intelligence. You, our Lord and our God, conquered our enemies, and made the lowliness of our weak nature to triumph through the abundant mercy of your grace.

   (*aloud*) And for all (your helps and graces towards us, let us raise to you praise and honour and thanksgiving and worship, now and ever and world without end). *People:* Amen.

*The priest says privately:* You, Lord, through your many mercies which cannot be told, be graciously mindful of all the pious and righteous fathers who were pleasing in your sight, in the commemoration of the body and blood of your Christ, which we offer to you on the pure and holy altar, as you taught us. And grant us your tranquillity and your peace for all the days of this age, (*Repeat.*) *People:* Amen. that all the inhabitants of the earth may know you, that you alone are the true God and Father, and you sent our Lord Jesus Christ, your beloved Son, and he, our Lord and our God, taught us through his life-giving gospel all the purity and holiness of the prophets, apostles, martyrs, confessors, bishops, priests, deacons, and all sons of the holy catholic Church who have been sealed with the living seal of holy baptism.

And we also, Lord (*thrice*), your lowly, weak and miserable servants, who have gathered and stand before you, and have received through tradition the form[1] which is from you, rejoicing, glorifying, exalting, commemorating, and celebrating this great mystery of the passion, death, and resurrection of our Lord Jesus Christ, may your Holy Spirit, Lord, come and rest on this offering of your servants, and bless and sanctify it, that it may be to us, Lord, for remission of debts, forgiveness of sins, and the great hope of resurrection from the dead, and new life in the kingdom of heaven, with all who have been pleasing in your sight.

And because of all your wonderful dispensation towards us, with open mouths and uncovered faces let us give you thanks and glorify you without ceasing in your Church, which has been redeemed by the precious blood of your Christ, offering up (praise, honour, thanksgiving and adoration to your living and life-giving name, now and at all times for ever and ever). *People:* Amen.

1. *Or* example *or* pattern.

# 7

# The Anaphora of Basil of Caesarea

This anaphora is extant in three forms:
1. In Coptic, lacking the first third of the anaphora.
2. In Coptic, with many additions to the text of no. 1.
3. In Greek, with further additions to the text of no. 2.

The text translated here is that of no. 2 up to the point where no. 1 begins, which is then followed to the end of the anaphora. No. 1 is translated from the French rendering by E. Lanne, no. 2 from the Latin translation by E. Renaudot.

In the first form, it may well have been brought to Egypt by St Basil *c.* A.D. 357, and thus represents the use of Cappadocia in the first half of the fourth century. If so, it is one of the earliest surviving anaphoras. Later it was amplified, probably by St Basil himself, into the Liturgy of St Basil (p. 83). Though showing signs of use in Egypt, it is Antiochene in structure.

BIBLIOGRAPHY

J. Doresse and E. Lanne, *Un témoin archaïque de la liturgie copte de saint Basile* (1960).

E. Renaudot, *Liturgiarum Orientalium Collectio* (1847), vol. 1, pp. 13–18.

*Prex Eucharistica*, pp. 347–57 (Greek text no. 3).

A. Houssiau, 'The Alexandrine Anaphora of St Basil', in L. C. Sheppard (ed.), *The New Liturgy* (1970), pp. 228–43.

*The bishop:*[1]  The Lord be with you.
*People:*  And with your spirit.
*Bishop:*  Lift up your hearts.
*People:*  We have them with the Lord.
*Bishop:*  Let us give thanks to the Lord.
*People:*  It is fitting and right.
*Bishop:*  It is fitting and right, fitting and right, truly it is fitting and right, I AM, truly Lord, God existing before the ages and reigning

1. Latin: *sacerdos.*

29

until the ages; you dwell on high and regard what is low; you made heaven and earth and the sea and all that is in them. Father of our Lord and God and Saviour Jesus Christ, through whom you made all things visible and invisible, you sit on the throne of your glory; you are adored by every holy power. Before you stand angels and archangels, principalities and powers, thrones, dominions, and virtues; around you stand the Cherubim with many eyes and the Seraphim with six wings, for ever singing the hymn of glory and saying:

*People:* Holy, holy, holy, Lord of Sabaoth (etc).

*Bishop:* Holy, holy, holy, you are indeed, Lord our God. You formed us and placed us in the paradise of pleasure; and when we transgressed your commandment through the deceit of the serpent, and fell from eternal life, and were banished from the paradise of pleasure, you did not cast us off for ever, but continually visited us through your holy prophets; and in these last days you manifested to us who sat in darkness and the shadow of death your only-begotten Son, our Lord and God and Saviour, Jesus Christ. He was made flesh of the Holy Spirit and of the holy virgin Mary, and became man; he showed us the ways of salvation, granted us to be reborn from above by water and the Spirit, and made us a people for his own possession, sanctifying us by his Holy Spirit. He loved his own who were in the world, and gave himself for our salvation to death who reigned over us and held us down because of our sins.

  **2.** . . . by his blood. From the cross he descended into hell and rose from the dead the third day, he ascended into heaven and sat at the right hand of the Father; he appointed a day on which he will judge the world with justice and render to each according to his works.

  And he left us this great mystery of godliness: for when he was about to hand himself over to death for the life of the world, he took bread, blessed, sanctified, broke, and gave it to his holy disciples and apostles, saying, 'Take, eat from this, all of you; this is my body, which is given for you and for many for forgiveness of sins. Do this for my remembrance.'

  Likewise also the cup after supper: he mixed wine and water, blessed, sanctified, gave thanks, and again gave it to them, saying,

2. The earliest Coptic text begins here.

'Take, drink from it, all of you; this is my blood which is shed for you and for many for forgiveness of sins. Do this for my remembrance. For as often as you eat this bread and drink this cup, you proclaim my death until I come.'

We also, remembering his holy sufferings, and his resurrection from the dead, and his return to heaven, and his session at the right hand of the Father, and his glorious and fearful coming (again), have set forth before you your own from your own gifts, this bread and this cup. And we, sinners and unworthy and wretched, pray you, our God, in adoration that in the good pleasure of your goodness your Holy Spirit may come upon us and upon these gifts that are set before you, and may sanctify them and make them holy of holies.

Make us worthy to partake of your holy things for sanctification of soul and body, that we may become one body and one spirit, and may have a portion with all the saints who have been well-pleasing to you from eternity.

Remember, Lord, also your one, holy, catholic, and apostolic Church: give it peace, for you purchased it with the precious blood of Christ; and all the orthodox bishops in it.

Remember first of all your servant Archbishop Benjamin and his colleague in the ministry holy Bishop Colluthus, and all who with him dispense the word of truth: grant them to feed your holy churches, your orthodox flocks, in peace.

Remember, Lord, the priests and all the deacons and assistants, all those in virginity and chastity, and all your faithful people; and have mercy on them.

Remember, Lord, also this place, and those who live in it in the faith of God.

Remember, Lord, also the weather and the fruits of the earth.

Remember, Lord, those who offer these gifts to you, and those for whom they presented them; and grant them all a heavenly reward.

Since, Master, it is a command of your only-begotten Son that we should share in the commemoration of your saints, vouchsafe to remember, Lord, also those of our fathers who have been well-pleasing to you from eternity: patriarchs, prophets, apostles, martyrs, confessors, preachers, evangelists, and all the righteous perfected in faith; especially the holy and glorious Mary, Mother of God and ever-virgin, through whose prayers have mercy on us all, and save us through your holy name which has been invoked upon us.

Remember likewise all those of the priesthood who have already died, and all those of lay rank; and grant them rest in the bosom of Abraham, Isaac and Jacob, in green pastures, by waters of comfort, whence pain, sorrow, and sighing have fled away.

*The deacon reads the diptychs.*

*Bishop:* Give them rest in your presence; preserve us who live here in your faith, guide us to your kingdom, and grant us your peace at all times; through Jesus Christ and the Holy Spirit. The Father in the Son, the Son in the Father with the Holy Spirit, in your one, holy, catholic Church.

# 8

# Sarapion: *The Euchologion*

A collection of prayers attributed to Sarapion, bishop of Thmuis in the Nile Delta *c.* A.D. 340–60, is preserved on Mount Athos. This attribution, however, has been challenged on the ground that much of the phraseology of the prayers is Arian in character, whereas Sarapion was a friend of Athanasius. Even so, the anaphora must date from a period when the intercessions (apart from the memorial of the dead) were still at an earlier point in the service, and not included within the anaphora itself. The opening paragraphs show also that the celebrant still retained considerable freedom in the content of his thanksgiving. Paragraphs 10–13 have probably been interpolated from the Liturgy of St Mark (pp. 47–8); they exhibit the characteristic Egyptian bridge-passage after the Sanctus, based on the words 'full' and 'fill'.

The contents of the collection do not appear to be arranged in the proper order, and the table below follows F. E. Brightman's rearrangement.

BIBLIOGRAPHY

F. E. Brightman, 'The Sacramentary of Serapion of Thmuis', in *Journal of Theological Studies*, I (1900), pp. 88–113.
*Prex Eucharistica*, pp. 128–33.
Dix, *The Shape*, pp. 162–72.
Bouyer, pp. 203–8.

FIRST PRAYER OF SUNDAY (19)
PRAYER AFTER RISING FROM THE SERMON (20)
PRAYER FOR THE CATECHUMENS (21)
BLESSING[1] OF THE CATECHUMENS (28)
PRAYER FOR THE PEOPLE (27)
BLESSING[1] OF THE PEOPLE (29)
PRAYER FOR THE SICK (22)
BLESSING[1] OF THE SICK (30)

1. Greek: *cheirothesia* (laying-on of hands).

### PRAYER OF OFFERING OF BISHOP SARAPION (1)

It is fitting and right to praise, to hymn, to glorify you, the uncreated Father of the only-begotten Jesus Christ.

We praise you, uncreated God, unsearchable, ineffable, incomprehensible by all created being.

We praise you who are known by the only-begotten Son, who were spoken of through him and interpreted and made known to created nature.

We praise you who know the Son and reveal to the saints the glories about him, who are known by your begotten Word, and seen and interpreted to the saints.

We praise you, unseen Father, provider of immortality: you are the fountain of life, the fountain of light, the fountain of all grace and all truth, lover of man and lover of the poor; you reconcile yourself to all and draw all to yourself through the coming of your beloved Son.

We pray you: make us living men.

Give us a spirit of light, that we may know you, the true (God) and him whom you have sent, Jesus Christ.

Give us holy Spirit, that we may be able to speak and expound your unspeakable mysteries.

May the Lord Jesus Christ speak in us, and holy Spirit, and hymn you through us.

For you are far above every principality and power and virtue and every name that is named, not only in this age but in the age to come.

Beside you stand thousands of thousands and myriads of myriads of angels, archangels, thrones, dominions, principalities, and powers. Beside you stand the two most honourable seraphim with six wings, which cover the face with two wings, and the feet with two, and fly with two; and they cry, 'Holy'.

With them receive also our cry of 'Holy', as we say: 'Holy, holy, holy, Lord of Sabaoth; heaven and earth are full of your glory.'

Full is heaven, full also is earth of your excellent glory, Lord of the powers. Fill also this sacrifice with your power and your partaking; for to you have we offered this living sacrifice, this bloodless offering.

To you have we offered this bread, the likeness of the body of the only-begotten. This bread is the likeness of the holy body. For the Lord Jesus Christ, in the night when he was betrayed, took bread, broke it, and gave it to his disciples, saying, 'Take and eat; this is my body which is broken for you for forgiveness of sins.'

Therefore we also, making the likeness of the death, have offered the bread, and beseech you through this sacrifice: be reconciled to us all and be merciful, O God of truth. And as this bread was scattered over the mountains, and was gathered together and became one, so gather your holy Church out of every nation and every country and every city and village and house, and make one living catholic Church.

We have offered also the cup, the likeness of the blood: for the Lord Jesus Christ, taking a cup after supper, said to his disciples, 'Take, drink; this is the new covenant, which is my blood, which is shed for you for the forgiveness of sins.' Therefore we have offered the cup also, presenting the likeness of the blood.

O God of truth, let your holy Word come on this bread, that the bread may become body of the Word; and on this cup, that the cup may become blood of the Truth; and make all who partake to receive a medicine of life for the healing of every disease, and for strengthening of all advancement and virtue; not for condemnation, O God of truth, and not for censure and reproach.

For we have called upon you, the uncreated, through the only-begotten, in holy Spirit. Let this people receive mercy; let it be counted worthy of advancement; let angels be sent out to be present among the people for bringing to naught the evil one, and for confirmation of the Church.

And we entreat also for all who have fallen asleep, of whom is the remembrance.

*After the recitation of the names:* Sanctify these souls, for you know them all; sanctify all the souls that are fallen asleep in the Lord, and number them with all your holy powers, and give them a place and a mansion in your kingdom.

Receive also the thanksgiving of the people, and bless those who offered the offerings and the thanksgivings;[2] and grant health and soundness and cheerfulness and all advancement of soul and body to this whole people.

Through your only-begotten Jesus Christ in holy Spirit; as it was and is and shall be to generations of generations and to all the ages of ages.

Amen.

FRACTION AND PRAYER DURING THE FRACTION (2)
Make us worthy of this communion also, God of truth, and make our bodies receive purity, and our souls insight and knowledge; and make us wise, God of compassion, by participation in the body and the blood; for through the only-begotten are glory and might to you in holy Spirit, now and to all the ages of ages. Amen.

BLESSING[3] OF THE PEOPLE AFTER THE COMMUNION OF THE CLERGY (3)
PRAYER AFTER THE COMMUNION OF THE PEOPLE (4)

PRAYER OVER THE OFFERINGS OF OILS AND WATERS (5)
We bless these created things through the name of your only-begotten Jesus Christ; we name the name of him who suffered, was crucified, rose again, and sits at the right hand of the uncreated, on this water and oil. Grant healing power to these created things, that every fever and every demon and every disease may be driven away by drinking and anointing; and the partaking of these created things be a healing medicine and a medicine of wholeness; in the name of your only-begotten Jesus Christ, through whom be glory and might to you in holy Spirit, to all the ages of ages. Amen.

BLESSING[3] AFTER THE BLESSING[4] OF WATER AND OIL (6)

---

2. *i.e., the bread and the wine.*
3. Greek: *cheirothesia* (laying-on of hands).        4. Greek: *eulogia.*

# 9

# Early Egyptian Fragments

The four texts translated below have all been recovered during the present century.

The first (Strasbourg, gr. 254) is a papyrus of the fourth or fifth centuries, which shows the anaphora of St Mark in its earliest known form.

The second (British Museum, 54036) is a Coptic version on a wooden tablet of the second half of the anaphora. Though written in the eighth century, it represents an earlier form of the text, confirmed by a sixth-century parchment of the same extract in Greek (Manchester, Rylands Library 465), which is however much less complete.

The third is a papyrus from Deir Balyzeh in Upper Egypt (Oxford, MS Gr. Lit. d 2–4 P), of the sixth or seventh century; and the fourth a papyrus in Coptic, no longer extant (Louvain, Coptica 27). These two may well share a common ancestor with St Mark, but they have a consecratory epiclesis before the Institution Narrative.

Words in brackets have been supplied from the Liturgy of St Mark, and may be taken as certain. Conjectural restorations are followed by a question mark; dots represent a gap which might be filled in more than one way.

BIBLIOGRAPHY
a. M. Andrieu & P. Collomp, 'Fragments sur papyrus de l'anaphore de saint Marc', in *Revue des Sciences Religieuses*, 8 (1928), pp. 489–515.
*Prex Eucharistica*, pp. 116–19.
b. H. Quecke, 'Ein saidischer Zeuge der Markusliturgie (Brit. Mus. 54.036)', in *Orientalia Christiana Periodica*, 37 (1971), pp. 40–54.
c. C. H. Roberts, *Catalogue of the Greek and Latin Papyri in the John Rylands Library*, 3 (1938), no. 465, pp. 25–8.
*Prex Eucharistica*, pp. 120–3.
C. H. Roberts & B. Capelle, *An Early Euchologium* (1949).
*Prex Eucharistica*, pp. 124–7.
d. L. Th. Lefort, 'Coptica lovanensia', in *Le Muséon*, 53 (1940), pp. 1–66, no. 27.
*Prex Eucharistica*, p. 140.

## a. The Strasbourg Papyrus

[1] to bless (you) . . . (night) and day . . .

(you who made) heaven (and) all that is in (it, the earth and what is on earth,) seas and rivers and (all that is) in (them); (you) who made man (according to your) own image and likeness. You made everything through your wisdom, your true light, your Son, our Lord and Saviour Jesus Christ, through whom with him and the Holy Spirit we give thanks to you and offer this reasonable and bloodless service, which all the nations offer you, from sunrise to sunset, from south to north, (for) your name is great among all the nations, and in every place incense is offered to your holy name and a pure sacrifice.

Over this sacrifice and offering we pray and beseech you, remember your holy and only catholic Church, all your peoples and all your flocks. Provide the peace which is from heaven in all our hearts, and grant us also the peace of this life. The . . . of the land peaceful things towards us, and towards your (holy) name, the leader of the . . . , the army, the princes, councils, . . .

(*About one-third of a page is lacking here, and what survives is too fragmentary in places to be restored.*)

for harvest . . . preserve, for the poor of (your) people, for all of us who call upon (your) name, for all who trust in you. Give rest to the souls of those who have fallen asleep; remember those of whom we make mention today, both those whose names we say (and) whose we do not say . . . our orthodox holy fathers and bishops everywhere; and grant us to have a part and lot with the fair . . . of your holy prophets, apostles, and martyrs. Receive(?) . . . their entreaties . . . grant them through our Lord, through whom be glory to you to the ages of ages.

1. Cf. pp. 43–5.

## b. The British Museum Tablet

[2] Full in truth are heaven and earth of your glory through our Lord (and) Saviour Jesus Christ: fill, O God, this sacrifice also with your blessing through your Holy Spirit. For our Lord and Saviour and King of all, Jesus Christ, in the night when he was betrayed and willingly underwent death, took bread in his holy and undefiled (and) blessed hands, looked up to heaven to you, the Father of all, blessed, gave thanks over it, sanctified, broke (and) gave it to his disciples (and) apostles, saying, 'Take and eat of this, all of you; this is my body, which is given for you for the forgiveness of your sins. Do this for my remembrance.'

Likewise, after supper, he took a cup, blessed, sanctified, (and) gave it to them, saying, 'Take this and drink of it, all of you; this is my blood of the new covenant, which is shed for many for the forgiveness of their sins. Do this for my remembrance. For as often as you eat this bread and drink this cup, you proclaim my death (and) confess my resurrection.'

Proclaiming thus, Lord, the death of your only-begotten Son, our Lord and Saviour Jesus Christ, and confessing his resurrection and his ascension into heaven, and looking for his glorious coming, we offer before you these gifts from your own, this bread and this cup. We pray and beseech you to send your Holy Spirit and your power on these (your?) (gifts) set before you, on this bread and this cup, and to make the bread the Body of Christ and (the cup the blood of the) new (covenant) of our Lord and Saviour Jesus Christ.

2. Cf. pp. 48–9.

## c. The Deir Balyzeh Papyrus

[3] . . . who hate . . . bless (your) people . . . raise the fallen, turn back the wanderers, comfort the weak-hearted.

For you are above every principality and power and virtue and every name that is named, not only in this age but also (in the age to come). By (you) stand (thousands) of the holy (angels and) (unnumbered) . . . the . . . stand in a circle . . . (six) wings to one and six to the other, and with two they veiled the face, and with two the feet, and with two they flew. Everything at all times hallows you, but with all that hallow you, receive also our hallowing, as we say to you: Holy, holy, holy, Lord of Sabaoth; heaven and earth are full of your glory. Fill us also with the glory from (you), and vouchsafe to send down your Holy Spirit upon these creatures (and) make the bread the body of our (Lord and) Saviour Jesus Christ, and the cup the blood . . . of our Lord and . . . And as this bread was scattered on (the mountains) and hills and fields, and was mixed together and became one body . . . so this wine which came from the vine of David and the water from the spotless lamb also mixed together became one mystery, so gather the catholic Church . . .

For (our Lord Jesus) Christ himself, (in the night when) he handed (himself) over . . . his disciples (and) apostles, saying, 'Take . . . from it; this (is) my body, which is given for you for forgiveness of sins.' Likewise after supper he took the cup, blessed, drank, and gave it to them, saying, 'Take, drink; this is my blood, which is shed for you for forgiveness of sins. As often as you eat this bread and drink this cup, you proclaim my death, you make my remembrance.'

We proclaim your death, we confess your resurrection and we pray . . .

(*At least fifteen lines are missing here.*)

. . . and provide us your servants with the power of the Holy Spirit, for strengthening and increasing of faith, for the hope of the eternal life to come; through our Lord Jesus Christ, (with whom) be glory to you, the Father, with the Holy (Spirit) to the ages. Amen.

3 Cf. pp. 47–9.

## d. The Louvain Coptic Papyrus

**⁴**. . . earth of your glory. Heaven and earth are full of that glory wherewith you glorified us through your only-begotten Son Jesus Christ, the first-born of all creation, sitting at the right hand of your majesty in heaven, who will come to judge the living and the dead. We make the remembrance of his death, offering to you your creatures, this bread and this cup. We pray and beseech you to send out over them your Holy Spirit, the Paraclete, from heaven . . . to make (?) the bread the body of Christ, and the cup the blood of Christ of the new covenant.

Thus the Lord himself, when he was soon to be betrayed, took bread, gave thanks over it, blessed it, broke it, and gave it to the disciples, and said to them: 'Take, eat, for this is my body which will be given for you.' Likewise after supper, he took the cup also, gave thanks over it, and gave it to them, saying: 'Take, drink, for this is my blood which will be shed for many for forgiveness (of sins)' . . .

4. Cf. p. 48.

# 10

# The Liturgy of St Mark

The liturgy of the patriarchate of Alexandria in its final, thirteenth-century form exhibits a rite to which substantial additions had been made from the liturgies of St Basil and St James. An early edition of this rite appears in a Coptic translation (Anaphora of St Cyril) made soon after A.D. 451. This lacks certain elements which appear in the later Greek text. But it is possible to reconstruct an almost complete anaphora of an even earlier date by piecing together early Greek and Coptic fragments.

The characteristic structure of Egyptian anaphoras has the Intercessions inserted into the middle of the Preface, and an epiclesis to link the Sanctus to the Institution Narrative.

The text translated below is that of the oldest complete manuscript, written at Rossano in Southern Italy in the thirteenth century; words and phrases absent from the Coptic are in square brackets. The early fragments may be found on pp. 37–41.

BIBLIOGRAPHY
*Prex Eucharistica*, pp. 101–15 (Greek), 135–9 (Coptic).
*L.E.W.*, pp. 113–43 (Greek), 144–88 (Coptic).
R. G. Coquin, 'L'anaphore alexandrine de saint Marc', in B. Botte *et al*, *Eucharisties d'Orient et d'Occident* (1970), vol. 2, pp. 51–82.
Bouyer, pp. 209–14.

ENARXIS (THREE PRAYERS)
  THE LITTLE ENTRANCE
PRAYER, HYMN, PRAYER OF THE TRISAGION
EPISTLE
ALLELUIA AND PRAYER OF CENSING
GOSPEL
PRAYERS OF THE FAITHFUL (LITANY)

THE GREAT ENTRANCE
CHERUBIC HYMN
KISS OF PEACE
NICENE CREED
PRAYER OF PROTHESIS

THE ANAPHORA

*Likewise after the Creed the bishop[1] seals[2] the people and says aloud:*
        The Lord be with all.
*People:*    And with your spirit.
*Bishop:*    Up with your hearts.[3]
*People:*    We have them with the Lord.
*Bishop:*    Let us give thanks to the Lord.
*People:*    It is fitting and right.
*Deacon:*    Spread (the fans).

*The bishop begins the anaphora:* It is truly fitting and right, holy and suitable, and profitable to our souls, [I AM,] Master, Lord, God, Father Almighty, to praise you, to hymn you, to give thanks to you, to confess you night[4] and day with [unceasing mouth,] unhushed lips, and unsilenced heart; you who have made heaven and what is in heaven, the earth and what is on earth, seas, springs, rivers, lakes and all that is in them; you who made man according to your own image and likeness, [and granted him the pleasure of paradise. When he transgressed, you did not despise him or abandon him, for you are good, but you called him back through the law, you taught him through the prophets, you reformed and renewed him through this awesome and life-giving and heavenly mystery.] You made everything through your wisdom, the true light, your only Son, our Lord and God and Saviour, Jesus Christ, through whom with him and the Holy Spirit we give thanks to you and offer this reasonable and bloodless service, which all the nations offer you, [Lord,] from sunrise to sunset, from south to north, for your name is great among all the nations, and in every place incense is offered to your holy name [5]and a pure sacrifice, a sacrifice and offering.

    And we pray and beseech you[5], for you are good and love mankind:

---

1. Greek: *hiereus.*      2. *i.e. makes the sign of the cross over them.*
3. *The Greek has no verb.*      4. Cf. p. 38.
5. *The Coptic reads:* . . . and a pure sacrifice. And over this sacrifice and this offering we pray and beseech you . . . *This is supported by the Strasbourg papyrus.*

remember, Lord, the holy and only catholic and apostolic Church from one end of the earth to the other, all your peoples and all your flocks.

Provide the peace which is from heaven in all our hearts, and grant us also the peace of this life.

Dispose the emperor, the army, the princes, councils, townships, neighbourhoods, our goings-out and our comings-in in all peace.

King of peace, give us your peace, for you have given us everything; possess us, Lord, in concord and love; we know none but you, we name your name. Give life to all our souls, and let not the death of sin prevail against us and all your people.

Visit, Lord, the sick among your people and in mercy and pity heal them. Drive away from them and from us every disease and illness; expel the spirit of weakness [from them.] Raise up those who have lain in lengthy illnesses, heal those that are troubled by unclean spirits. Have mercy on all those who are held in prison, or in the mines, [under accusation or condemnation,] in exile, or bitter slavery [or tribute], and free them all. For you are [our God,] who loosens the bonds, who restores the broken, the hope of the hopeless, the help of the helpless, [the raising-up of the fallen,] the harbour of the storm-tossed, [the avenger of the afflicted.] To every afflicted and hard-pressed [Christian] soul give mercy, give relief, give refreshment. And also, Lord, heal the diseases of our souls, and cure our bodily weaknesses, healer of souls and bodies. Overseer of all flesh, oversee [and heal] us through your salvation.

Give a good journey to our brothers who have gone abroad or are going abroad in every place, whether by land or by river, on lakes or on roads, or travelling by any means; bring them all back from everywhere to a quiet harbour, to a safe harbour; vouchsafe to sail and to journey with them; return them rejoicing to their rejoicing families, in health to healthy families. And also, Lord, keep our sojourn in this life free from harm and storm until the end.

[Send the good rains richly on the places that ask for them and need them; by their falling, cheer and renew the face of the earth, that by their drops it may spring up rejoicing.]

Bring up the waters of the river to their proper measure; [by their rising] cheer [and renew] the face of the earth; water its furrows, multiply its crops.

[Bless, Lord, the fruits of the earth; keep us safe and unharmed;] grant them to us for seedtime and harvest, [that by their drops it may spring up rejoicing.]

Bless, Lord, the crown of the year of your goodness, for the poor of your people, for the widow and the orphan, for the stranger and the proselyte, for all of us who trust in you and call upon your holy name; for the eyes of all hope for you, and you give their food in due season. You who give food to all flesh, fill our hearts with joy and gladness, that we may always have all sufficiency and abound to every good work [in Christ Jesus our Lord.]

[King of kings and Lord of lords,] guard the kingdom of your servant [our orthodox and Christ-loving emperor, whom you appointed to rule over the land] in peace and bravery and righteousness. Subject to him, O God, every warlike enemy [at home and] abroad. [Lay hold upon the weapon and buckler and stand up to help him; bring forth the broadsword and stop the way against them that persecute him; set the fruit of his loins upon his throne;] speak to his heart good things concerning your holy, catholic, and apostolic Church [and all the Christ-loving people,] that we may live a quiet and peaceful life in his peace, that we may be found in all godliness and honesty towards you.

Give rest [Lord our God,] to the souls of our fathers and brothers who have fallen asleep [in the faith of Christ,] remembering our forefathers from the beginning, the fathers, patriarchs, prophets, apostles, martyrs, confessors, bishops, [holy men,] righteous men, every spirit perfected in the faith [of Christ], and those of whom we make mention today, and our holy father Mark the apostle and evangelist, [who showed us the way of salvation.]

[Hail, highly favoured, the Lord is with you, blessed are you among women, and blessed is the fruit of your womb, for you bore the Saviour of our souls.]

*Aloud:* Especially our all-holy, [spotless, blessed Lady] Mary, Mother of God and ever-virgin.

[*Deacon:* Bless, Lord.

*Bishop:* The Lord bless you with his grace, now and always, and to the ages of ages.]

*The deacon reads the diptychs of the departed.*

*The bishop bows and prays:* Give rest, Master, Lord our God, to the souls of all these [in the tabernacle of your saints in your kingdom,] granting them the good things of your promises, which eye has not seen nor ear heard neither have entered into the heart of man what God has prepared for those that love your holy name. Refresh their souls and count them worthy of the kingdom of heaven; and grant the ends of our lives to be Christian and well-pleasing [and sinless,] and give us to have a part and lot with all your saints.

Receive, O God, the thank-offerings of those who offer the sacrifices, at your [holy and] heavenly and intellectual altar in the vastnesses of heaven by the ministry of your archangels; of those who offered much and little, secretly and openly, willingly but unable, and those who offered the offerings today; as you accepted the gifts of your righteous Abel, (*the bishop censes and says*) the sacrifice of our father Abraham, [the incense of Zachariah, the alms of Cornelius,] and the widow's two mites; receive also their thank-offerings, and give them imperishable things for perishable, heavenly things for earthly, eternal for temporal.

The most holy and blessed pope N. whom you foreknew and foreordained to govern your holy, catholic, and apostolic Church, and our most holy bishop N., preserve, preserve them for many years to complete in peaceful times your holy pontificate, entrusted to them by you according to your holy and blessed will, rightly dividing the word of truth.

Remember also the orthodox bishops, presbyters, deacons, subdeacons, readers, singers, monks, virgins, widows, laymen everywhere.

[Remember, Lord, the holy city of Christ our God, and the imperial city, and this our city, and every city and land and those who dwell in them in the orthodox faith of Christ, for their peace and safety.

Remember, Lord, every Christian soul in trials and afflictions, in need of the mercy and help of God, and recovery of the lost.

Remember, Lord, those of our brothers who are prisoners of war; grant them to find pity from those who took them prisoner.

Remember, Lord, in mercy and pity us sinners also, your unworthy servants, and wipe away our sins, as a good God who loves mankind.

Remember, Lord, also me your humble and sinful and unworthy servant, and wipe away my sins as one that loves mankind; and be present with us who minister to your all-holy name.]

Bless our meetings, Lord; root out idolatry altogether from the world; tread down Satan and all his work and wickedness under our feet. Humble now as always, Lord, the enemies of your Church; strip them of their arrogance; show them quickly how weak they are; render harmless their plots and devices and schemings which they contrive against us. Arise, Lord, and let your enemies be scattered, and all who hate your holy name flee backwards; but bless[6] your faithful and orthodox people who do your [holy] will, to thousands of thousands and myriads of myriads.

*Deacon:* Those who are seated, stand.

*The bishop says the prayer:* Ransom the prisoners, rescue those in necessity, feed the hungry, comfort the weak-hearted, turn back the wanderers, [enlighten those in darkness,] raise the fallen, strengthen the unstable, [heal the sick,] lead all into the way of salvation, and gather them in your holy fold; but save us from our law-breaking, as our guard and defender in everything.

*Deacon:* Look eastwards.

*The bishop bows and prays:* You are above every principality and power and virtue and dominion and every name that is named, not only in this age but in the age to come. Beside you stand thousands of thousands and myriads of myriads of armies of holy angels and archangels. Beside you stand your two most honourable living creatures, the cherubim with many eyes and the seraphim with six wings, which cover their faces with two wings, and their feet with two, and fly with two; and they cry one to the other with unwearying mouths and never-silent doxologies, singing, proclaiming, praising, crying, and saying the triumphal and thrice-holy hymn to your magnificent glory: Holy, holy, holy, Lord of Sabaoth; heaven and earth are full of your holy glory. (*aloud*) Everything at all times hallows you, but with all that hallow you receive also, Lord and Master, our hallowing, as with them we hymn you and say:

6. Cf. p. 40.

*People:* Holy, holy, holy, Lord of Sabaoth; heaven and earth[7] are full of your holy glory.

*The bishop seals the holy things and says:* Full[8] in truth are heaven and earth of your holy glory through [the appearing of] our Lord and God and Saviour Jesus Christ: fill, O God, this sacrifice also with a blessing from you through the descent of your [all-]holy spirit. For our Lord and God and King of all, Jesus the Christ, in the night when he handed himself over for our sins, and underwent death [in the flesh] for all men [sat down with his holy disciples and apostles, he] took bread in his holy, undefiled, and blameless hands, looked up to heaven to you, his own Father, the God [of us and] of all men, gave thanks, blessed, sanctified, broke, and gave it to his holy [and blessed] disciples and apostles, saying: (*aloud*) 'Take, eat,

(*Deacon:* stretch forth, presbyters.)

this is my body, which is broken for you and given for the forgiveness of sins.'

*People.* Amen.

*The bishop says privately:* Likewise also after supper he took the cup, he mixed wine and water, [looked up to heaven to you, his own Father, the God of us and of all men] gave thanks, blessed and sanctified it, [filled it with the Holy Spirit,] and gave it to his holy and blessed disciples and apostles, saying: (*aloud*)

'Drink from it, all of you;

(*Deacon:* still stretch forth.)

this is my blood of the new covenant, which is shed for you and for many, and given for the forgiveness of sins.' *People:* Amen.

*The bishop prays thus:* 'Do this for my remembrance. For as often as you eat this bread and drink this cup, you proclaim my death and confess my resurrection [and ascension] until I come.'

Proclaiming, [Master,] Lord, Almighty, [heavenly King,] the death of your only-begotten Son, our Lord and God and Saviour Jesus Christ, and [confessing] his blessed resurrection [from the dead on the third day] and his ascension into heaven and his session at your right hand, his God and Father, and looking for his second [and dread and awesome] coming, in which he will judge the living and the dead in

7. Cf. p. 40.        8. Cf. pp. 38–40.

righteousness and to reward each according to his works [– spare us, Lord our God –] we have offered before you from your own gifts; and we pray and beseech you, for you are good and love man, send out from your holy height, from your prepared dwelling-place, from your unbounded bosom, the Paraclete himself, the Holy Spirit of truth, the Lord, the life-giver, who spoke through the law and prophets and apostles, who is present everywhere and fills everything, who on his own authority and not as a servant works sanctification on whom he wills, in your good pleasure; single in nature, multiple in action, the fountain of divine endowments, consubstantial with you, proceeding from you, sharing the throne of the kingdom with you and your only-begotten Son, our Lord and God and Saviour, Jesus Christ; [look] upon us and ⟨ ?send⟩ upon these loaves and these cups your Holy Spirit to sanctify and consecrate them, [as Almighty God,] (*aloud*) and make the bread the body, *People:* Amen: *The bishop aloud:* and the cup the blood of the new covenant of our Lord and God and Saviour and King of all, Jesus Christ,

(*Deacon:* Descend, deacons; pray, presbyters.)

that they may become to all of us who partake of them for faith, for sobriety, for healing, [for temperance, for sanctification,] for renewal of soul, body, and spirit, for fellowship in eternal life and immortality, for the glorifying of your [all-]holy name, for forgiveness of sins; that in this as in everything your all-holy and honourable and glorified name may be glorified and praised and sanctified, with Jesus Christ and the Holy Spirit.

*People:* As it was and is and shall be, to generation and generation, and to all the ages of ages. Amen.


PRAYER AND LORD'S PRAYER
PRAYER OF INCLINATION


PRAYER OF ELEVATION
*The bishop, aloud:* The holy things to the holy people.
*People:* One Father is holy, one Son is holy, one Spirit is holy, in the unity of the Holy Spirit. Amen.

COMMUNION

*The bishop:* The holy body of our Lord and God and Saviour Jesus Christ.

The precious blood of our Lord and God and Saviour Jesus Christ.

THANKSGIVING FOR COMMUNION AND PRAYER
DISMISSAL

# II

# Cyril of Jerusalem: *Lectures*

The passages below are taken from the *catecheses* (lectures to candidates for baptism) traditionally ascribed to St Cyril, bishop of Jerusalem *c.* A.D. 349–86. The last five lectures (*catecheses mystagogicae*) were delivered after the Easter baptism, those on the eucharist on Thursday and Friday of Easter week, in the Anastasis, a church built over the Holy Sepulchre. 'The bishop stands leaning against the inner screen . . . and interprets all that takes place.'[1]

If Cyril is indeed the author, the lectures will have been delivered *c.* 350; but many modern scholars accept the attribution made in several manuscripts to John II, Cyril's successor as bishop. In this case, the lectures cannot be earlier than 387, a period which seems more appropriate from the doctrinal point of view. The rite on which the author comments has affinities with both Egyptian and Syrian liturgies.

BIBLIOGRAPHY

F. L. Cross, *St Cyril of Jerusalem: Lectures* (1951).

E. J. Yarnold, *The Awe-Inspiring Rites of Initiation* (1972), pp. 88–95.

A. A. Stephenson, *The Works of St Cyril of Jerusalem* (Fathers of the Church, vol. 64) (1970), pp. 143–203.

W. Telfer, *Cyril of Jerusalem and Nemesius of Emesa* (Library of Christian Classics, vol. 4) (1955), pp. 19–63.

G. J. Cuming, 'Egyptian Elements in the Jerusalem Liturgy', in *Journal of Theological Studies*, n.s. 25 (1974), pp. 117–24.

## Lecture 4, The Body and Blood of Christ

1    This teaching of blessed Paul is sufficient to give you full assurance about the divine mysteries of which you have been deemed worthy, so that you have become one body and one blood with Christ. For he has just affirmed,

1. J. D. Wilkinson, *Egeria's Travels* (1971), p. 145.

That in the night when he was betrayed our Lord Jesus Christ took bread, and when he had given thanks, he broke it and gave it to his disciples, saying, 'Take, eat; this is my body.'

And taking a cup and giving thanks, he said, 'Take, drink; this is my blood.'

Since he himself has declared and said of the bread, 'This is my body,' who will thereafter dare to doubt? And since he has strongly affirmed and said, 'This is my blood,' who will ever doubt, saying that it is not his blood?

3   So we partake with all assurance as of the body and blood of Christ. For in the figure of bread his body is given to you, and in the figure of wine his blood; that, by partaking of the body and blood of Christ, you may become one body and one blood with him . . .

5   There was also in the Old Testament the shewbread; but, since it was of the Old Testament, it came to an end. But in the New Testament there is heavenly bread and a cup of salvation, sanctifying soul and body. For as the bread corresponds to the body, so the Word accords with the soul.

7   . . . You see here the cup referred to, which Jesus took in his hands, gave thanks, and said, 'This is my blood, which is shed for many for forgiveness of sins.'

## Lecture 5, The Eucharist

2   You saw the deacon giving the ablutions to the bishop[2] and to the presbyters who surround the altar of God . . .

3   Then the deacon cries, 'Receive one another and let us greet one another.' . . .

4   After this, the bishop cries, 'Up with your hearts,'[3]
Then you answer, 'We have them with the Lord.' . . .

5   Then the bishop says, 'Let us give thanks to the Lord.'
Then you say, 'It is fitting and right.'

6   After this, we make mention of heaven and earth and sea; of sun and moon and stars; of all creation, rational and irrational, visible and invisible; of angels, archangels, virtues, dominions, principalities, powers, thrones; of the Cherubim with many faces; saying with full

2. Greek: *hiereus*.     3. The Greek has no verb.

effect the (words) of David, 'Magnify the Lord with me.' We make mention also of the Seraphim, whom Isaiah saw in the Holy Spirit standing in a circle round the throne of God, with two wings veiling the face, and with two the feet, and with two flying, and saying, 'Holy, holy, holy (is the) Lord of Sabaoth.'

That is why we say this hymn of praise[4] which has been handed down to us from the Seraphim, that we may share with the heavenly armies in their hymnody.

7   Then, having sanctified ourselves with these spiritual hymns, we beseech God, the lover of man, to send forth the Holy Spirit upon (the gifts) set before him, that he may make the bread the body of Christ, and the wine the blood of Christ; for everything that the Holy Spirit has touched, has been sanctified and changed.

8   Then, after the spiritual sacrifice, the bloodless service, has been perfected, we beseech God over that sacrifice of propitiation, for the common peace of the churches, for the stability of the world, for emperors, for armies and auxiliaries, for those in sickness, for the oppressed; and praying in general for all who need help, we all offer this sacrifice.

9   Then we make mention also of those who have fallen asleep; first patriarchs, prophets, apostles, martyrs; that through their prayers and advocacy God may receive our supplication. Then also for the holy fathers and bishops who have fallen asleep, and indeed for all who have fallen asleep before us; for we believe that there will be a very great profit to the souls for whom supplication is offered in the presence of the holy and most dread sacrifice.

## 10   AN ILLUSTRATION

### 11–18   EXPOSITION OF THE LORD'S PRAYER

11   Then, after that, we say that prayer which the Saviour handed down to his own disciples, with a clear conscience addressing God as Father and saying, 'Our Father in heaven' . . .

18   . . . Then, when the prayer is finished, you say, 'Amen', which means 'So be it'; thus you set the seal on the contents of this prayer taught us by God.

4. Reading *doxologian*; other readings are: *theologian* and *homologian.*

19    After this, the bishop says, 'The holy things for the holy people.'

Holy are the things set forth, for they have received the coming of the Holy Spirit; holy also are you, for you have been deemed worthy of the Holy Spirit. The holy things correspond to the holy people.

Then you say, 'One is holy, one is Lord, Jesus Christ.'

For truly one is holy, holy by nature; but if we are holy, we are not so by nature, but by communion and discipline and prayer.

20    After this, you hear the chanter inviting you with a divine melody to the communion of the holy mysteries, and saying, 'Taste and see that the Lord is good.'

Do not entrust judgment to your bodily palate, but to undoubting faith; for what you taste is not bread and wine, but the likeness of the body and blood of Christ.

21    When you approach, do not come with your hands stretched or your fingers separated; but make your left hand a throne for the right, since it is to receive a king. Then hollow your palm and receive the body of Christ, saying after it, 'Amen.' Carefully sanctify your eyes by the touch of the holy body, then partake, taking care not to lose any of it . . .

22    Then, after having partaken of the body of Christ, approach also the cup of his blood. Do not stretch out your hands, but, bowing and saying 'Amen' in a gesture of adoration and reverence, sanctify yourself by partaking of the blood of Christ also. While the moisture is still on your lips, touch it with your hands and sanctify your eyes and forehead and the other senses. Then wait for the prayer, and give thanks to God who has deemed you worthy of such great mysteries.

23  **DOXOLOGY**

# 12

# The Liturgy of St James

This liturgy, which belongs to the Antiochene family, is especially associated with Jerusalem. It has several points of contact with the *Catecheses* of Cyril of Jerusalem (pp. 51–4), and it seems probable that it is the result of conflating the earlier liturgies of Antioch and Jerusalem, perhaps about the year 400. Subsequently it was much influenced by the liturgy of St Basil, and in its turn influenced the Liturgy of St Mark. A Syriac translation probably made soon after the Council of Chalcedon (A.D. 451) lacks a number of phrases (in square brackets below) which may be assumed to be later additions, while making substantial additions of its own.

The text translated below is that of Vatican MS gr. 2282, dating from the ninth century, which originated in the neighbourhood of Damascus. The text printed by Brightman is a fourteenth-century manuscript from Thessalonica (Paris Bibl. Nat. gr. 2509), in which the Intercession is much shorter.

BIBLIOGRAPHY

*Prex Eucharistica*, pp. 244–61 (Vatican text), 269–75 (Syriac).

*L.E.W.*, pp. 31–68 (Greek), 69–110 (Syriac).

Bouyer, pp. 268–80.

A. Tarby, *La prière eucharistique de l'église de Jérusalem* (1972).

M. H. Shepherd, 'Eusebius and the Liturgy of St James', in *Yearbook of Liturgical Studies*, 4 (1963), pp. 109–25.

PROTHESIS (TWO PRAYERS)

ENARXIS (FIVE PRAYERS)

   THE LITTLE ENTRANCE

PRAYER AND SYNAPTE (LITANY)

ANTIPHON AND EPISTLE

ALLELUIA AND TWO PRAYERS

GOSPEL

PRAYERS OF THE FAITHFUL (LITANY)
  THE GREAT ENTRANCE
CHERUBIC HYMN
FIVE PRAYERS
NICENE CREED
KISS OF PEACE
TWO OFFERTORY PRAYERS AND TWO PRAYERS OF THE VEIL

THE ANAPHORA

*The bishop:*[1]  The love of God the Father, the grace of our Lord [and] God and Saviour Jesus Christ, and the fellowship [and the gift] of the [all-]holy Spirit be with you all.

*People:*  And with your spirit.

*The bishop:*  Let us lift up our mind and our hearts.

*People:*  We have them with the Lord.

*The bishop:*  Let us give thanks to the Lord.

*People:*  It is fitting and right.

*The bishop, bowing, says:* It is truly fitting and right, suitable and profitable, to praise you, [to hymn you,] to bless you, to worship you, to glorify you, to give thanks to you, the creator of all creation, visible and invisible, [the treasure of eternal good things, the fountain of life and immortality, the God and Master of all.] You are hymned by [the heavens and] the heaven of heavens and all their powers; the sun and moon and all the choir of stars; earth, sea, and all that is in them; the heavenly Jerusalem, [the assembly of the elect,] the church of the first-born written in heaven, [the spirits of righteous men and prophets, the souls of martyrs and apostles;] angels, archangels, thrones, dominions, principalities and powers, and awesome virtues. The cherubim with many eyes and seraphim with six wings, which cover their own faces with two wings, and their feet with two, and fly with two, cry one to the other with unwearying mouths and never-silent doxologies, (*aloud*) [singing] with clear voice the triumphal hymn of your magnificent glory, proclaiming, praising, crying, and saying:

*People:* Holy, holy, holy, Lord of Sabaoth; heaven and earth are full of your glory. Hosanna in the highest. Blessed is he that comes and will come in the name of the Lord. Hosanna in the highest.

1. Greek: *hiereus.*

*And the bishop, standing up, seals the gifts, saying privately:* Holy you are, King of the ages, and [Lord and] Giver of all holiness; holy too is your only-begotten Son, our Lord Jesus Christ, [through whom you made all things;] and holy too is your [all-]holy Spirit, who searches out all things, even your depths, O God [and Father.] And he bows and says: Holy you are, almighty, omnipotent, awesome, good, [compassionate,] with sympathy above all for your fashioning. You made man from the earth [after your image and likeness,] and granted him the enjoyment of paradise; and when he transgressed your commandment and fell, you did not despise him or abandon him, for you are good, but you chastened him as a kindly father, you called him through the law, you taught him through the prophets.

Later you sent your only-begotten Son, our Lord Jesus Christ, into the world to renew [and raise up] your image [by coming himself.] He came down [from heaven] and was made flesh from the Holy Spirit and Mary, the holy [ever-]virgin Mother of God. He dwelt among men and ordered everything for the salvation of our race.

And when he was about to endure his voluntary [and life-giving] death [on the cross,] the sinless for us sinners, in the night when he was betrayed,[2] [or rather handed himself over,[2]] for the life and salvation of the world,

*Then he stands up, takes the bread, seals it, and says:* he took bread in his holy, undefiled, blameless [and immortal] hands, [looked up to heaven and] showed it to you, his God and Father; he gave thanks, blessed, sanctified, and broke it, and gave it to his [holy and blessed] disciples and apostles, saying,

*And he puts the bread down, saying aloud:* 'Take, eat; this is my body, which is broken and distributed for you for forgiveness of sins.' *People:* Amen.

*Then he takes the cup, seals it, and says privately:* 'Likewise after supper [he took] the cup, he mixed wine and water, [he looked up to heaven and showed it to you, his God and Father; he gave thanks,] blessed, and sanctified it, [filled it with the Holy Spirit,] and gave it to his [holy and blessed] disciples and apostles, saying,

*And he puts it down, saying aloud:* 'Drink from it, all of you; this is my

2. Greek: *paredidoto* and *paredidou.*

blood of the new covenant, which is shed and distributed for you and for many for forgiveness of sins.' *People:* Amen.

*Then he stands and says privately:* 'Do this for my remembrance; for as often as you eat this bread and drink this cup, you proclaim the death of the Son of Man [and confess his resurrection,] until he comes.'

*And the deacons present answer:* We believe and confess.

*People:* Your death, Lord, we proclaim and your resurrection we confess.

*Then he makes the sign of the cross, bows, and says:* We [sinners,] therefore, [also] remembering [his life-giving sufferings and his saving cross and] his death [and his burial] and his resurrection from the dead on the third day and his return to heaven and his session at your right hand, his God and Father, and his glorious and awesome second coming, when he comes [with glory] to judge the living and the dead, when he will reward each according to his works [ – spare us, Lord our God (*thrice*) – or rather according to his own compassion,] we offer you, [Master,] this awesome and bloodless sacrifice, [asking you] that you deal not with us after our sins nor reward us according to our iniquities, but according to your gentleness and [unspeakable] love for man to [pass over and] blot out [the handwriting that is against us[3]] your suppliants, [and grant us your heavenly and eternal gifts, which eye has not seen nor ear heard nor have entered into the heart of man, which you, O God, have prepared for those who love you. And do not set at nought your people on account of me and my sins, O Lord, lover of men (*thrice*),]

(*aloud*) for your people and your Church entreats you.

*People:* Have mercy on us, [Lord, God,] Father, the Almighty.

*And the bishop stands up and says privately:* Have mercy on us, Lord, God, Father, the Almighty; [have mercy on us, God, our Saviour. Have mercy on us, O God, according to your great mercy,] and send out upon us and upon these holy gifts set before you your [all-]holy Spirit, (*he bows*) the Lord and giver of life, who shares the throne and the kingdom with you, God the Father and your [only-begotten] Son, consubstantial and co-eternal, who spoke in the law and the prophets and your new covenant, who descended in the likeness of a dove upon our Lord Jesus Christ in the river Jordan [and remained upon him,] who

3. *Syriac:* the sins of.

descended upon your holy apostles in the likeness of fiery tongues [in the Upper Room of the holy and glorious Zion on the day of the holy Pentecost; *he stands up and says privately:* send down, Master, your all-holy Spirit himself upon us and upon these holy gifts set before you,] (*aloud*) that he may come upon them, [and by his holy and good and glorious coming may sanctify them,] and make this bread the holy body of Christ, *People:* Amen. And this cup the precious blood of Christ, *People:* Amen.

*The bishop stands up and says privately:* that they may become to all who partake of them for forgiveness of sins and for eternal life, for sanctification of souls and bodies, for bringing forth good works, for strengthening your holy, [catholic, and apostolic] Church, which you founded on the rock of faith, that the gates of hell should not prevail against it, rescuing it from every heresy, and from the stumbling-blocks of those who work lawlessness, [and from the enemies who rose and rise up] until the consummation of the age.

*The clerics alone answer:* Amen.

*Then he makes the sign of the cross, bows, and says:* We offer to you, [Master,] for your holy places also, which you glorified by the theophany of your Christ [and the descent of your all-holy Spirit;] principally for [holy and glorious] Zion, the mother of all the churches, and for your holy, [catholic, and apostolic] Church throughout all the world: even now, Master, grant it richly the gifts of your [all-]holy Spirit.

Remember, Lord, also our holy [fathers and] bishops [in the Church,] who [in all the world] divide the word of truth in orthodoxy; principally our holy father N., all his clergy and priesthood: grant him an honourable old age; preserve him to shepherd your flock in all piety and gravity for many years.

Remember, Lord, the honourable presbytery here and everywhere, the diaconate in Christ, all the other assistants, every ecclesiastical order, [our brotherhood in Christ, and all the Christ-loving people.

Remember, Lord, the priests who stand around us in this holy hour, before your holy altar, for the offering of the holy and bloodless sacrifice; and give them and us the word in the opening of our mouths to the glory and praise of your all-holy name.]

Remember, Lord, according to the multitude of your mercy and your pity, me also your humble, sinful and unworthy servant, and visit me in mercy and pity; save me and deliver me from those who persecute me, Lord, Lord of hosts; and since sin abounded in me, your grace shall greatly exceed it.

[Remember, Lord, also the deacons who surround your holy altar, and grant them a blameless life; preserve their ministry[4] unspotted and provide for them good degrees.

Remember, Lord, our God, your holy and royal city, and every city and region, and those who live in them in orthodox faith and reverence for you, for their peace and safety.]

Remember, Lord, our most pious [and Christ-loving] emperor, his pious [and Christ-loving] empress, [all his court and his army, for their help from heaven and their victory:] lay hold upon weapon and buckler, and stand up to help him; subject to him all [5]the warlike and barbarous nations that delight in war[5]; [moderate his counsels,] that we may lead a quiet and peaceful life in all piety and gravity.

Remember, Lord, [Christians at sea, on the road, abroad], our fathers and brothers in chains and prisons, in [captivity and] exile, [in mines and tortures and bitter slavery; for a peaceful return home for each of them.

Remember, Lord, those in old age and infirmity, those who are sick, ill, or troubled by unclean spirits, for their speedy healing and salvation by you, their God.

Remember, Lord, every Christian soul in trials and afflictions, in need of your mercy and help, O God, and recovery of the lost.

Remember, Lord, our holy fathers and brothers who live in chastity, piety, and self-discipline, and those who struggle among mountains, dens, and caves of the earth, and the orthodox communities everywhere, and our community in Christ here.

Remember, Lord, our fathers and brothers who labour and serve for your holy name.

Remember, Lord, all men for good; on all have mercy, Master; reconcile us all, bring peace to the multitudes of your people, disperse the scandals, abolish wars, end the divisions of the churches, speedily put down the uprisings of the heresies, cast down the insolence of the

4. Greek: *diakonia*.      5. *Syriac:* his enemies.

heathen, exalt the horn of the Christians, grant us your peace and your love, God our saviour, the hope of all the ends of the earth.]

Remember, Lord, mildness of climate, peaceful showers, good dews, abundance of fruit, a perfect harvest, and the crown of the year [of your goodness]; for the eyes of all wait upon you, and you give their food in due season; you open your hand and fill every living thing with blessing. (*Here he nods towards the archdeacon*) Remember, Lord, [those who have brought and bring forth fruit in your holy churches, O God, and remember the poor, and] those who have bidden us make mention of them in our prayers.

Vouchsafe yet to remember, Lord, those who have offered the offerings today on your holy altar, and those for whom each one offered or whom he has in mind, and those who are now read to you.[6] *And he makes mention of those whom he wishes who are in this present life.*

[Remember, Lord, also our parents and friends and relations and brothers NN.

Remember all these, Lord, whom we have remembered and these we have not remembered, of the orthodox; give them heavenly things for earthly, imperishable for perishable, eternal for temporal, according to the promise of your Christ, since you have authority over life and death.]

Vouchsafe yet to remember, Lord, those who have been well-pleasing to you from the beginning, [from generation to generation:] the holy fathers, patriarchs, prophets, apostles, [martyrs, confessors, holy teachers, and every righteous spirit perfected in the faith of your Christ.

Hail, highly favoured; the Lord is with you; blessed are you among women, and blessed is the fruit of your womb, for you bore the Saviour of our souls. (*thrice*)]

*He says aloud:* [Especially our all-] holy and blessed [Lady] Mary mother of God [and ever-virgin. *And the clergy alone answer secretly:* Remember, Lord, our God.] *And the bishop bows down and says:* Holy John, the [prophet,] forerunner and baptist.

[The holy apostles Peter, Paul, Andrew, James, John, Philip, Bartholomew, Thomas, Matthew, James, Simon, Jude, Matthias; Mark and Luke, the evangelists.

6. Or *recognized by you.*

The holy prophets and patriarchs and righteous men.

Holy Stephen, the first deacon and first martyr.

The holy martyrs and confessors, who for Christ our true God witnessed and confessed the good confession.

The infants who were put to death by King Herod.

The holy martyrs Procopius, Theodore, Cyrus, John, George, Leontius, Sergius, Bacchus, Cosmas, Damian, Sabinianus, Paul, Babilas, Agathangelus, Eustratius and his fellow-fighters.

The holy forty, the holy forty-five.

Holy Thecla, the first woman martyr.

The holy women who brought the myrrh.

The holy women martyrs Tatte, Febronia, Anastasia, Euphemia, Sophia, Barbara, Juliana, Irene, Faith, Hope, and Charity.]

Remember, Lord God our holy [fathers and] archbishops who, from [holy] James the apostle and brother of the Lord and first archbishop down to [7]Leo and Athanasius, have been orthodox archbishops of the holy city of Christ our Lord.[7]

[And those who have been archbishops from the beginning, from our holy and blessed father Eneas, an apostolic man and first of the bishops down to Sophronius and John.

Remember, Lord, our holy fathers and teachers Clement, Timothy, Ignatius, Dionysius, Irenaeus, Gregory, Alexander, Eustathius, Athanasius, Basil, Gregory, Gregory,[8] Ambrose, Amphilochius, Liberius, Damasus, John, Epiphanius, Theophilus, Celestinus, Augustine, Cyril, Leo, Proclus, Proterius, Philix, Hormisdas, Eulogius, Ephraem, Anastasius, Theodore, Martin, Agathon, Sophronius.

Remember, Lord, the six holy, great and ecumenical councils: the three hundred and eighteen (fathers) of Nicaea, and the one hundred and fifty of Constantinople, and the two hundred of the first Ephesus, and the six hundred and thirty of Chalcedon, and the one hundred and sixty-four of the fifth holy council, and the two hundred and eighty-nine of the sixth holy council, and the other holy councils and bishops who in all the world in orthodoxy divided the word of truth.

7. *Syriac:* the present day have preached the word of the orthodox faith in your holy churches.

8. i.e. Gregory of Nazianzus and Gregory of Nyssa.

Remember, Lord, our holy fathers and ascetics Paul, Antony, Charito, Paul, Pachomius, Hamoun, Theodore, Hilarion, Arsenius, Macarius, Macarius, Sisoius, John, Pambo, Poemen, Nilus, Isidore, Ephrem, Symeon, Symeon, Theodosius, Saba, Saba, Euthymius, Theoctistus, Gerasimus, Pantaleon, Maximus, Anastasius, Cosmas, John.

Remember, Lord, our holy fathers who were put to death by the barbarians in the holy mountain of Sinai and in Raitho, and our other holy fathers and orthodox ascetics and all the saints; not that we are worthy to make mention of their blessedness, but that they themselves indeed, standing by your awesome and dread judgment-seat, may make mention in turn of our misery.]

Remember, Lord, presbyters, deacons, deaconesses, subdeacons, readers, exorcists, interpreters, singers, monks, virgins, [widows, orphans, the continent, those who have been perfected with faith in the fellowship of your holy, catholic, and apostolic Church.

Remember, Lord, the pious and faithful emperors Constantine, Helena, Theodosius the Great, Marcianus, Pulcheria, Leo, Justinian, Constantine, and those who reigned after them in piety and faith,] and all the orthodox [Christ-loving] laymen who now sleep in the faith [and seal] of Christ.

[Remember, Lord, our parents and friends and relations.]

*And after them he makes mention of those orthodox whom he wishes.*

Remember all these orthodox, Lord, the God of the spirits and of all flesh, whom we have remembered and whom we have not remembered; give them rest yourself there, [in the land of the living, in your kingdom, in the pleasure of paradise,] in the bosom of Abraham, Isaac and Jacob, [our holy fathers,] whence pain, sorrow, and sighing have fled away, where the light of your countenance looks on them and lights them for ever. Guide the ends of our lives to be Christian [and well-pleasing] and sinless [in peace, Lord]; collect us under the feet of your elect, when you will and as you will, but without shame and transgressions, through your only-begotten Son, our Lord and God and Saviour Jesus Christ, for he alone has appeared on earth without sinning.

[*The deacon:* And for the peace and stability of the whole world and the holy churches of God; and for those for whom each one has offered or whom he has in mind, and for the people that stand round, for all men and all women.]

*The bishop says aloud:* Through whom, [as a good God and a Master that loves men,] to us and them *People:* Remit, forgive, pardon, O God, our transgressions, voluntary and involuntary,

*The bishop alone says:*[9] By the grace and compassion and love for man of your Christ, with whom you are blessed and glorified with the all-holy and life-giving Spirit, now and always and to the ages of ages. Amen.[9]

PRAYER AND LORD'S PRAYER
PRAYER OF INCLINATION

PRAYER OF ELEVATION
*The bishop raises the gift and says:* . . . The holy things for the holy people.
*People:* One is holy, one is Lord, Jesus Christ, to the glory of God the Father, with the Holy Spirit; to him be glory for the ages of ages.

COMMUNION
TWO PRAYERS BEHIND THE AMBO
THANKSGIVING FOR COMMUNION
DISMISSAL

9. The Syriac has a different doxology, of Egyptian type.

# 13

# The Apostolic Constitutions, Book 8

*The Apostolic Constitutions* is a compilation dating from *c.* A.D. 375, edited by the author of the pseudo-Ignatian Epistles. It is a collection of standard works, such as the *Didascalia* and the *Didache*, adapted and expanded by the anonymous author. Book 8 contains a liturgy of Antiochene type attributed to St Clement of Rome, and sometimes referred to as 'the Clementine Liturgy'. This certainly draws on, and greatly expands, the anaphora of the *Apostolic Tradition* of Hippolytus, and probably also makes use of the litanies of the Antioch rite. It is the earliest *complete* liturgy to have survived. It enjoyed a high reputation in eighteenth-century England, where it was regarded as genuinely apostolic, but there is no evidence that it was ever in use. The editor appears to have been an Arian. The best manuscript (Vatican gr. 1506) contains a number of phrases which have been omitted from all other manuscripts as heretical. They are printed below in angle-brackets. Words in round brackets are added to make sense.

BIBLIOGRAPHY

*L.E.W.*, pp. 3–27 (lacks Arian readings).
*Prex Eucharistica*, pp. 82–95 (lacks Intercessions and Arian readings).
Bouyer, pp. 244–68.
C. H. Turner, 'Notes on the Apostolic Constitutions: The Compiler an Arian', in *Journal of Theological Studies*, 16 (1915), pp. 54–61.
W. E. Pitt, 'The Anamneses and Institution Narrative in the Liturgy of Apostolic Constitutions Book VIII', in *Journal of Ecclesiastical History*, 9 (1958), pp. 1–7.

READINGS (INCLUDING OLD TESTAMENT)

SERMON

DISMISSALS OF THE CATECHUMENS, THE POSSESSED, AND THE
    PENITENTS

PRAYERS OF THE FAITHFUL

KISS OF PEACE
OFFERTORY

THE ANAPHORA
*Then, after praying privately, the bishop[1] puts on a splendid robe and stands
at the altar with the priests, makes the sign of the cross on his forehead with
his hands, and says,*

The grace of Almighty God and the love of our Lord Jesus Christ
and the fellowship of the Holy Spirit be with you all.

*All say together:*   And with your spirit.
*The bishop:*   Up with your mind.
*All:*   We have it with the Lord.
*The bishop:*   Let us give thanks to the Lord.
*All:*   It is fitting and right.

*The bishop:*   It is truly fitting and right to praise you before all
things, essentially existing God, existing before created things, from
whom all fatherhood in heaven and on earth is named, alone un-
begotten, without beginning, without lord or master, lacking nothing,
provider of all good things, greater than every cause and origin, always
being in one and the same mode, from whom all things came into
being as their starting-point.

For you are knowledge, without beginning, eternal vision, un-
begotten hearing, untaught wisdom, first in nature, alone in existence,
too great to be numbered. You brought all things from non-existence
into existence through your only-begotten Son; and him you begat
without an intermediary before all ages by your will and power and
goodness, your only-begotten Son, the Word, God, living wisdom,
the firstborn of all creation, the angel of your great purpose, your
high-priest ⟨and notable worshipper⟩, king and lord of all rational and
sentient nature, who was before all, through whom are all.

For you, eternal God, made all things through him, and through him
you vouchsafe a fitting providence over everything. Through him you
granted existence, through him also a good existence; O God the
Father of your only-begotten Son, through him before all things you
made ⟨the heavenly powers,⟩ the cherubim and the seraphim, the ages
and the hosts, virtues and powers, principalities and thrones, archangels

1. Greek: *archiereus.*

and angels; and through him after all these things you made this visible world and all that is in it.

For you are he who set out heavens as a vault, and stretched it out as a screen, and established the earth on nothing by your sole intent; you fixed the firmament, and arranged night and day, you brought light out of your treasures, and by its contraction you brought on darkness to (give) rest to the living things that move in the world. You appointed the sun in heaven to begin the day and the moon to begin the night, and you inscribed the chorus of the stars in heaven to the praise of your magnificence.

You made water for drinking and cleansing, lifegiving air for breathing in and out, and for the production of sound through the tongue striking the air, and for hearing which is aided by it to receive the speech which falls upon it.

You made fire for comfort in darkness, for supplying our need, that we should be warmed and given light by it.

You divided the ocean from the land, and made the one navigable, the other fit to be trodden by our feet; you filled it with creatures small and great, tame and wild; you wove it a crown of varied plants and herbs, you beautified it with flowers and enriched it with seeds.

You constructed the abyss and set a great covering on it, the piled-up seas of salt water, and surrounded it with gates of finest sand; now you raise it with winds to the height of the mountains, now you level it to a plain; now you drive it to fury with a storm, now you soothe it with a calm, so that it gives an easy journey to travellers in ships.

You girdled the world that was made by you through Christ and flooded it with torrents, you watered it with ever-flowing springs and bound it round with mountains as an unshakable and most safe seat for the earth.

For you filled the world and adorned it with sweet-smelling and healing herbs, with many different living things, strong and weak, for food and for work, tame and wild, with hissing of reptiles, with the cries of varied birds, the cycles of the years, the numbers of months and days, the order of the seasons, the course of rain-bearing clouds for the production of fruits and the creation of living things, a stable for the winds that blow at your command, the multitude of plants and herbs.

And not only have you fashioned the world, but you have also made in it, the citizen of the world, displaying him as the [2]ornament of the world[2]. For you said in your wisdom, 'Let us make man in our image and likeness, and let him rule over the fish of the sea and the birds of the air.'

So also you made him from an immortal soul and a perishable body, the one from what is not, the other from the four elements. And you gave him in respect of the soul, logical reason, discernment between godliness and ungodliness, observance of good and evil, and in respect of the body, the five senses and the power of motion.

For you, almighty God, planted by Christ a garden eastward in Eden with adornment of every kind of plant for food, and in it, as in a costly home, you placed man; and in making him you gave him an inborn law, that he might have in himself and of himself the seeds of the knowledge of God.

And when you had brought him into the paradise of delight, you allowed him authority to partake of everything, and forbade him the taste of one thing alone, in the hope of better things, that, if he kept the commandment, he should receive immortality as a reward for that.

But when he neglected the commandment and tasted the forbidden fruit, by the deceit of the serpent and the counsel of the woman, you justly drove him out of the paradise; but in your goodness you did not despise him when he was utterly perishing, for he was the work of your hands, but you subjected creation to him, and granted him to provide food for himself by his own sweat and labours, while you caused everything to shoot and grow and ripen. And in time, after putting him to sleep for a short while, you called him to rebirth by an oath; and after destroying the limit of death, you promised him life after resurrection.

Nor was this all, but you poured out his descendants to a countless multitude; you glorified those who remained faithful to you, and punished those who rebelled against you; you accepted the sacrifice of Abel as being a righteous man, and rejected the gift of Cain, who slew his brother, as being a man accursed.

For you are he who fashions men and provides life and fills need and gives laws and regards those that keep them and punishes those who

2. *Kosmou kosmon*: the Greek word *kosmos* has both these meanings.

break them; he who brought the great Flood upon the earth because of the multitude of the ungodly, and saved righteous Noah in the ark with eight souls, the end of those who dwelt there, but the beginning of those who were to be; he who kindled the terrible fire against the five cities of Sodom, and turned a fruitful land into salt for the wickedness of them that dwell in it, and snatched holy Lot from the burning.

You are he who rescued Abraham from the godlessness of his forefathers and made him inheritor of the world; and revealed your Christ to him; he who chose Melchizedek to be high-priest of your service; who declared your long-suffering servant Job to be the victor over the devil, the origin of evil; who made Isaac the child of promise; who made Jacob the father of twelve sons, and his descendants to become a multitude, and brought him into Egypt with seventy-five souls.

You, Lord, did not despise Joseph but, as a reward of his chastity for your sake, gave him the rule over the Egyptians. You, Lord, because of your promises to their fathers, did not despise the Hebrews when they were oppressed by the Egyptians, but you punished the Egyptians and rescued them.

And when men destroyed the law of nature and thought that the creation had created itself, or honoured it more than they should, making it equal to you, God of all, you did not allow them to go astray, but revealed your holy servant Moses and through him gave them the written law in aid of nature, you showed that the creation was your work and expelled the error of polytheism. You glorified Aaron and his descendants with the honour of priesthood, you punished the Hebrews when they sinned, and received them when they turned back.

You avenged them on the Egyptians with the ten plagues, you divided the sea and led the Israelites through, you drowned and destroyed the pursuing Egyptians. You sweetened the bitter water with wood, you poured water from the precipitous rock, you rained manna from heaven, and quails as food from the air. (You set up) a pillar of fire for light by night and a pillar of cloud for shadow from the heat by day. You declared Joshua to be leader, you destroyed through him the seven nations of Canaanites, you parted Jordan, you dried up the rivers of Etham, you laid walls low without machines or human hands.

For all things glory be to you, almighty Lord. You are worshipped ⟨by every bodiless and holy order, by the Paraclete, and above all by your holy child[3] Jesus the Christ, our Lord and God, your angel and the chief general of your power, and eternal and unending high priest,⟩ by unnumbered[4] armies of angels, archangels, thrones, dominions, principalities, powers, virtues, eternal armies. The Cherubim and the six-winged Seraphim with two wings covering their feet, with two their heads, and with two flying, together with thousands of thousands of archangels and myriads of myriads of angels say unceasingly, never resting their voices:

*All the people say:* Holy, holy, holy (is the) Lord of Sabaoth; heaven and earth are full of his glory; blessed (is he) for ever. Amen.

*The bishop continues:* Truly are you holy and all-holy, most high and exalted above all for ever.

Holy also is your only-begotten Son, our Lord and God Jesus the Christ, who ministered to you, his God and Father, in all things, in the varieties of creation, and in appropriate forethought. He did not overlook the race of men as it perished; but after the law of nature and the warnings of the Law and the reproofs of the prophets and the guardianship of the angels, when they were violating the natural and the written law, and casting out of memory the Flood, the burning (of Sodom), the plagues of the Egyptians, and the slaughter of the Palestinians, and were all about to perish as never yet, it pleased him, by your counsel, who was maker of man to become man, the lawgiver to be under the law, the high-priest to be the sacrifice, the shepherd to be a sheep.

And he propitiated you, his God and Father, and reconciled you to the world, and freed all men from the impending wrath. He was born of a virgin, God the Word made in the flesh, the beloved Son, the firstborn of all creation, according to the prophecies spoken beforehand by him concerning himself, from the seed of David and Abraham, of the tribe of Judah. He who fashions all who are begotten was made in a virgin's womb; the fleshless became flesh; he who was begotten outside time was begotten in time.

He lived a holy life and taught according to the law; he drove away every disease and every sickness from men; he did signs and wonders among the people; he who feeds those who need food and fills all

3. Or *servant* (cf. *Didache*, p. 14).    4. Another reading is *orderly*.

things living with plenteousness partook of food and drink and sleep; he made known your name to those who did not know it; he put ignorance to flight; he re-kindled piety; he fulfilled your will; he accomplished the work which you gave him.

And when he had achieved all these things, he was seized by the hands of lawless so-called priests and high-priests and a lawless people, by betrayal through one who was diseased with wickedness. He suffered many things at their hands, endured all kinds of indignity by your permission, and was handed over to Pilate the governor. The Judge was judged and the Saviour was condemned; he who cannot suffer was nailed to the cross, he who is immortal by nature died, and the giver of life was buried, that he might free from suffering and rescue from death those for whose sake he came, and break the bonds of the devil and deliver men from his deceit.

And on the third day he rose from the dead, and after spending forty days with his disciples, he was taken up into heaven and sits at your right hand, his God and Father.

Remembering therefore what he endured for us, we give you thanks, almighty God, not as we ought but as we are able, and we fulfil his command.

For in the night he was betrayed, he took bread in his holy and blameless hands and, looking up to you, his God and Father, he broke it and gave it to his disciples, saying, 'This is the mystery of the new covenant: take of it, eat; this is my body which is broken for many for forgiveness of sins.'

Likewise also he mixed the cup of wine and water and sanctified it and gave it to them, saying, 'Drink from this, all of you; this is my blood which is shed for many for forgiveness of sins. Do this for my remembrance; for as often as you eat this bread and drink this cup, you proclaim my death, until I come.'

Remembering then his passion and death and resurrection from the dead, his return to heaven and his future second coming, in which he comes with glory and power to judge the living and the dead, and to reward each according to his works, we offer you, King and God, according to his commandment, this bread and this cup, giving you thanks through him that you have deemed us worthy to stand before you and to be your priests.

And we beseech you to look graciously upon these gifts set before you, O God who need nothing, and accept them in honour of your Christ; and to send down your Holy Spirit upon this sacrifice, the witness of the sufferings of the Lord Jesus, that he may make[5] this bread body of your Christ, and this cup blood of your Christ; that those who partake may be strengthened to piety, obtain forgiveness of sins, be delivered from the devil and his deceit, be filled with Holy Spirit, become worthy of your Christ, and obtain eternal life, after reconciliation with you, almighty Lord.

Further we pray to you, Lord, for your holy Church from one end of the world to the other, which you redeemed with the precious blood of your Christ, that you would guard it unshaken and sheltered until the consummation of the age; and for all bishops who rightly divide the word of truth.

And we entreat you also for my worthless self who offer to you, and for all the priesthood, for the deacons and all the clergy, that you would instruct them and fill them with Holy Spirit.

And we entreat you, Lord, for the Emperor and those in authority and all the army, that they may be peaceable towards us, that we may live the whole of our life in quietness and concord, and glorify you through Jesus Christ our hope.

And we offer to you also for all those who have been well-pleasing to you from everlasting: holy patriarchs, prophets, righteous apostles, martyrs, confessors, bishops, priests, deacons, subdeacons, readers, chanters, virgins, widows, laymen, and all whose names you know.

And we offer to you for this people, that you would make them a royal priesthood, a holy nation, to the praise of your Christ; for those in virginity and chastity, for the widows of the Church, for those in holy marriage and child-bearing, for the infants among your people, that you may make none of us a castaway.

And we ask you on behalf of this city and those who live in it, for those in illnesses, those in bitter slavery, those in exile, those whose goods have been confiscated, for sailors and travellers, that you would become the help of all, their aid and support.

And we entreat you for those that hate and persecute us for the sake

5. Greek: *apophēnēi.*

of your name, for those who are outside and have gone astray, that you would turn them to good and soften their hearts.

And we entreat you also for the catechumens of the Church, for those distressed by possession, and for those in penitence among our brothers, that you would perfect the first in the faith, and cleanse the second from the works of the devil, and receive the repentance of the third, and forgive them and us our transgressions.

And we offer to you also for good weather and an abundant harvest, that we may partake of the good things from you without lack, and unceasingly praise you, who give food to all flesh.

And we entreat you also for those who are absent for good cause, that you would preserve us all in piety, and gather us in the kingdom of your Christ, the God of all rational and sentient nature, our King, without change, without blame, without reproach.

For to you ⟨through him⟩ (is due) all glory, worship, and thanksgiving, ⟨and through you and after you to him in⟩[6] the Holy Spirit, now and always and to the ages of ages, unfailing and unending.
*And all the people say:* Amen.


INCLINATION (LITANY AND PRAYER OF BLESSING)


ELEVATION OF THE HOLY BREAD
*The bishop says to the people:* The holy things to the holy people.
*The people answer:* One is holy, one is Lord, Jesus Christ, to the glory of God the Father, blessed to the ages. Amen.

Glory to God in the highest, and peace on earth, goodwill among men.

Hosanna to the Son of David: blessed is he who comes in the name of the Lord.

God is Lord and is manifested to us: hosanna in the highest.


COMMUNION
*The bishop gives the offering, saying:* The body of Christ.
*And he who receives says:* Amen.

6. In *was later altered to* to the Father, the Son, and.

*The deacon takes the cup and gives it, saying:* The blood of Christ, the cup of life.
*And he who drinks says:* Amen.

**THANKSGIVING FOR COMMUNION**
**DISMISSAL (PRAYER FOR PROTECTION)**

# 14

# Theodore of Mopsuestia: *Lectures*

Theodore, a fellow-student with John Chrysostom in Antioch, became bishop of Mopsuestia in southern Asia Minor in A.D. 392. His baptismal *catecheses* resemble those of Cyril of Jerusalem, but are much lengthier. Though written in Greek, they have survived only in Syriac. From scattered sentences in them it is possible to piece together the structure and some of the wording of the liturgy Theodore used. It clearly belongs to the Antiochene family. The text below is translated from the French rendering by R. Tonnerre, and the numbers refer to the pages in his edition.

BIBLIOGRAPHY

R. Tonnerre & R. Devréesse, *Les homélies catéchétiques de Theodore de Mopsueste* (1949), pp. 513–605.

E. J. Yarnold, *The Awe-Inspiring Rites of Initiation* (1972), pp. 211–63.

Dix, *The Shape*, passim.

## Lecture 15

513 PROTHESIS (PRAYER AND THANKSGIVING)
521 KISS OF PEACE
527 ABLUTIONS
527 READING OF DIPTYCHS OF LIVING AND DEAD

## Lecture 16

529 *Deacon:* Behold the offering.

531 *Bishop:* The grace of our Lord Jesus Christ and the love of God the Father and the communion of the Holy Spirit be with you all.

*People:* And with your spirit.

*Bishop:* Up with your spirits.[1]

1. The Syriac has no verb.

*People:* To you, O Lord.

*Bishop:* Let us give thanks to the Lord.

*People:* It is fitting and right.

541 The bishop proclaims that all praise and glory are fitting for God, and that it is right for us to give him adoration and worship.

543 He speaks of the greatness of the Father and of the Son and of the Holy Spirit.

545 *Bishop:* Praise and adoration be offered to the divine nature by all creation,

543   and by the invisible powers (among them the Seraphim), and we say with them,

*People:* Holy, holy, holy, Lord of Sabaoth; heaven and earth are full of your praises.

549 *Bishop:* Holy is the Father, holy also the Son, holy also the Holy Spirit.

He speaks of the ineffable compassion which God showed in the dispensation through Christ, who, though he was in the form of God, was willing to accept the form of a servant, and put on perfect and complete man for the redemption of the whole human race.

551 Our Lord, when he was about to go to his passion, handed down to his disciples the immortal and spiritual food that we might receive it.

*Bishop:* But now our Lord Christ must rise from the dead by virtue of these actions and spread his grace over us.

553 The bishop must ask and beseech God that the Holy Spirit should come, and that grace should come thence upon the bread and wine offered, that they may be known to be truly the body and blood of our Lord, the memorial of immortality.

555 He prays that the grace of the Holy Spirit may come upon all gathered together, that they may be united as into one body by partaking of the body of our Lord... and that they may be one in concord, peace and welldoing.

He ends the liturgy by offering prayer for all whom it is our rule to mention in church at all times. Then he goes on to the commemoration of those who have died.

557 FRACTION

563 PRAYER FOR ACCEPTANCE OF THE SACRIFICE

565 *Bishop:* That which is holy for the holy people.

569 *People:* One Father alone is holy; one Son alone is holy; one Spirit alone is holy. Glory to the Father, to the Son, and to the Holy Spirit, to the ages of ages. Amen.

577 COMMUNION

579 *Bishop:* The body of Christ. *People:* Amen.

581 THANKSGIVING FOR COMMUNION

# 15

# The Liturgy of St John Chrysostom

This liturgy became, and has remained, the principal and normal rite of the Orthodox Church. Its structure is of the West Syrian type, with the epiclesis following the Institution Narrative and preceding the Intercessions. It may well have preserved the form used in Antioch during Chrysostom's episcopate (A.D. 370–98). Much of the language can be paralleled from his sermons, in which he often refers to the liturgy familiar to his hearers.

The text translated below is that of the Barberini manuscript, written at the end of the eighth century, with the people's part supplied from modern editions. As far as the anaphora is concerned, the contemporary form differs from the Barberini text only in a few additions from the Liturgy of St Basil, here in angle-brackets, and in the omission of two phrases, here in square brackets.

BIBLIOGRAPHY
*L.E.W.*, pp. 309–99, 470–81.
*Prex Eucharistica*, pp. 223–9.
A. Oakley, *The Orthodox Liturgy* (1958).
Bouyer, pp. 280–90.

PROTHESIS (PRAYER IN VESTRY)
ENARXIS (LITANY, THREE ANTIPHONS AND PRAYERS)[1]
   THE LITTLE ENTRANCE
PRAYERS OF ENTRANCE AND OF THE TRISAGION [PRAYER OF THE THRONE[2]]
FOUR HYMNS[1]
EPISTLE, PSALM, GOSPEL
EKTENĒ (PRAYER OF SUPPLICATION)
DISMISSAL OF CATECHUMENS, WITH PRAYER

  1. These items do not appear in the Barberini MS.    2. Later omitted.

PRAYERS OF THE FAITHFUL 1 AND 2
  THE GREAT ENTRANCE
CHERUBIC HYMN
PROSKOMIDĒ (PRAYER OF OFFERING)
KISS OF PEACE
NICENE CREED

THE ANAPHORA

*The priest says:*   The grace of our Lord Jesus Christ, and the love of the God and Father, and the fellowship of the Holy Spirit be with you all.

*People:*   And with your spirit.

*Priest:*   Let us lift up our hearts.

*People:*   We have them with the Lord.

*Priest:*   Let us give thanks to the Lord.

*People:*   It is fitting and right ⟨to worship the Father, the Son, and the Holy Spirit, the consubstantial and undivided Trinity⟩.

*The priest begins the holy anaphora:* It is fitting and right to hymn you, ⟨to bless you, to praise you,⟩ to give you thanks, to worship you in all places of your dominion. For you are God, ineffable, inconceivable, invisible, incomprehensible, existing always and in the same way, you and your only-begotten Son and your Holy Spirit. You brought us out of not-being to being; and when we had fallen, you raised us up again; and did not cease to do everything until you had brought us up to heaven, and granted us the kingdom that is to come. For all these things we give thanks to you and to your only-begotten Son and to your Holy Spirit, for all that we know and do not know, your seen and unseen benefits that have come upon us. We give you thanks also for this ministry; vouchsafe to receive it from our hands, even though thousands of archangels and ten thousands of angels stand before you, cherubim and seraphim, with six wings and many eyes, flying on high (*aloud*) singing the triumphal hymn ⟨proclaiming, crying, and saying:⟩

*People:* Holy, ⟨holy, holy, Lord of Sabaoth; heaven and earth are full of your glory. Hosanna in the highest. Blessed is he who comes in the name of the Lord. Hosanna in the highest.⟩

*The priest, privately:* With these powers, O Master, lover of man, we also cry and say: holy are you and all-holy, and your only-begotten Son, and your Holy Spirit; holy are you and all-holy and magnificent is your glory; for you so loved the world that you gave your only-begotten Son that all who believe in him should not perish, but have eternal life.

When he had come and fulfilled all the dispensation for us, on the night in which he handed himself over, he took bread in his holy and undefiled and blameless hands, gave thanks, blessed, broke and gave it to his holy disciples and apostles, saying, (*aloud*) 'Take, eat; this is my body, which is ⟨broken⟩ for you ⟨for forgiveness of sins⟩. ⟨*People:* Amen.⟩ Likewise the cup also after supper, saying, (*aloud*) 'Drink from this, all of you; this is my blood of the new covenant, which is shed for you and for many for the forgiveness of sins.'
*People:* Amen.
*The priest, privately:* We therefore, remembering this saving commandment and all the things that were done for us: the cross, the tomb, the resurrection on the third day, the ascension into heaven, the session at the right hand, the second and glorious coming again; (*aloud*) offering you your own from your own, in all and through all,
*People:* we hymn you, ⟨we bless you, we give you thanks, O Lord and pray to you, our God.⟩
*The priest says privately:* We offer you also this reasonable and bloodless service, and we beseech and pray and entreat you, send down your Holy Spirit on us and on these gifts set forth; and make this bread the precious body of your Christ, [changing it by your Holy Spirit, Amen; and that which is in this cup the precious blood of your Christ, changing it by your Holy Spirit,] Amen;
*The priest privately:* so that they may become to those who partake for vigilance of soul, for forgiveness of sins, for fellowship with the Holy Spirit, for the fullness of the kingdom ⟨of heaven⟩, for boldness towards you; not for judgment or for condemnation.

We offer you also this reasonable service for those who rest in faith, ⟨forefathers⟩, fathers, patriarchs, prophets, apostles, preachers, evangelists, martyrs, confessors, ascetics, and all the righteous ⟨spirits⟩ perfected in faith; (*aloud*) especially our all-holy, immaculate, highly glorious, blessed Lady, Mother of God and ever-virgin Mary; Saint John the ⟨prophet,⟩ forerunner and Baptist, and the holy ⟨glorious⟩

and honoured apostles; and this saint whose memorial we are keeping, and all your saints: at their entreaties, look upon us, O God.

And remember all those who have fallen asleep in hope of resurrection to eternal life, and grant them rest where the light of your own countenance looks upon them.

Again we beseech you, remember, Lord, all the orthodox episcopate who rightly divide the word of your truth, all the priesthood, the diaconate in Christ, and every order of the clergy.

We offer you this reasonable service also for the (whole) world, for the holy, catholic, and apostolic Church, for those who live in a chaste and reverend state, [for those in mountains and in dens and in caves of the earth,] for the most faithful Emperor, the Christ-loving Empress, and all their court and army: grant them, Lord, a peaceful reign, that in their peace we may lead a quiet and peaceful life in all godliness and honesty.

Remember, Lord, the city in which we dwell, and all cities and lands, and all who dwell in them in faith.

(*aloud*) Above all, remember, Lord, our Archbishop N.

Remember, Lord, those at sea, those travelling, the sick, those in adversity, prisoners, and their salvation.

Remember, Lord, those who bring forth fruit and do good works in your holy churches and remember the poor; and send out your mercies upon us all,

(*aloud*) and grant us with one mouth and one heart to glorify and hymn your all-honourable and magnificent name, the Father, the Son, and the Holy Spirit, now and always and to the ages of ages.
*People:* Amen.

PRAYER AND LORD'S PRAYER
PRAYER OF INCLINATION

PRAYER OF ELEVATION
*The priest raises the holy bread and says:* The holy things for the holy people.
*People:* One is holy, one is Lord, Jesus Christ, to the glory of God the Father.

COMMUNION
THANKSGIVING FOR COMMUNION
DISMISSAL (PRAYER BEHIND THE AMBO)

# 16

# The Liturgy of St Basil

Like the Liturgy of St John Chrysostom, the Liturgy of St Basil is in current use in the Orthodox Church, but on only ten days in the year. The anaphora is a highly developed version of the Anaphora of Basil of Caesarea (p. 29). Parallels have been found in the writings of St Basil (d. A.D. 379), and he is generally believed to have added the numerous scriptural quotations. The structure is of the Antiochene type, with an unusually long post-sanctus section. At several points the wording is very similar to, or identical with, that of the Liturgy of St John Chrysostom, which this anaphora has probably influenced.

The text below is translated from the Barberini manuscript, written at the end of the eighth century, as far as the Institution Narrative, at which point there is a lacuna which has been filled below from the Grottaferrata manuscript ΓB vii (ninth or tenth century). The Barberini manuscript begins again towards the end of the Intercession. Later additions are in angle-brackets, later omissions in square brackets.

BIBLIOGRAPHY

*L.E.W.*, pp. 309–44, 400–11, 521–6.

*Prex Eucharistica*, pp. 230–43.

A. Oakley, *The Orthodox Liturgy* (1958).

Bouyer, pp. 290–303.

W. E. Pitt, 'The Origin of the Anaphora of the Liturgy of St Basil', in *Journal of Ecclesiastical History*, 12 (1961), pp. 1–13.

PROTHESIS (PRAYER IN VESTRY)

ENARXIS (THREE ANTIPHONS AND PRAYERS)

   THE LITTLE ENTRANCE

PRAYERS OF ENTRANCE AND OF THE TRISAGION, [PRAYER OF
   THE THRONE[1]]

READINGS AND CHANTS

EKTENĒ (PRAYER OF SUPPLICATION)

  1. Later omitted.

DISMISSAL OF CATECHUMENS, WITH PRAYER
PRAYERS OF THE FAITHFUL 1 AND 2
  THE GREAT ENTRANCE
PRAYER OF THE CHERUBIC HYMN
PROSKOMIDĒ (PRAYER OF OFFERING)
KISS OF PEACE
NICENE CREED

THE ANAPHORA

*Priest:* The grace of our Lord Jesus Christ and the love of the God and Father, and the fellowship of the Holy Spirit be with you all.

*People:* And with your spirit.

*Priest:* Let us lift up our hearts.

*People:* We have them with the Lord.

*Priest:* Let us give thanks to the Lord.

*People:* It is fitting and right ⟨to worship the Father, the Son, and the Holy Spirit, the consubstantial and undivided Trinity⟩.

*And the priest begins the holy anaphora:* I AM, Master, Lord God, Father almighty, reverend, it is truly fitting and right and befitting the magnificence of your holiness to praise you, to hymn you, to bless you, to reverence you, to give you thanks, to glorify you, the only truly existing God, and to offer to you with a contrite heart and a humble spirit this our reasonable service. For you are he who granted us the knowledge of your truth; and who is sufficient to declare your powers, to make all your praises to be heard, or to tell of all your wonders at all times? [Master,] Master of all, Lord of heaven and earth and all creation, visible and invisible, you sit on the throne of glory and behold the depths, without beginning, invisible, incomprehensible, infinite, unchangeable, the Father of our Lord Jesus Christ the great God and saviour of our hope, who is the image of your goodness, the identical seal, manifesting you the Father in himself, living Word, true God, before all ages wisdom, sanctification, power, the true Light by whom the Holy Spirit was revealed, the spirit of truth, the grace of sonship, the pledge of the inheritance to come, the first fruits of eternal good things, lifegiving power, the fountain of sanctification, by whose enabling the whole reasonable and intelligent creation does you service and renders you unending praise and glory; for all things are your servants. For angels, archangels, thrones, dominions, principalities, powers, virtues, and the cherubim with many eyes praise you, the seraphim stand around you, each having six wings, and with two covering their own faces, and with two their feet, and with two flying, and crying one to the other with unwearying mouths and never-silent doxologies, (aloud) singing the triumphal hymn, crying aloud and saying:

People: Holy, ⟨holy, holy, Lord of Sabaoth; heaven and earth are full of your glory. Hosanna in the highest. Blessed is he who comes in the name of the Lord. Hosanna in the highest.⟩

The priest says privately: With these blessed powers, O Master, lover of men, we sinners also cry and say: you are truly holy and all-holy, and there is no measure of the magnificence of your holiness, and you are holy in all your works, for in righteousness and true judgment you brought all things upon us. For you took dust from the earth and formed man; you honoured him with your image, O God, and set him in the paradise of pleasure, and promised him immortality of life and enjoyment of eternal good things in keeping your commandments. But when he had disobeyed you, the true God who created him, and had been led astray by the deceit of the serpent, and had been subjected to death by his own transgressions, you, O God, expelled him in your righteous judgment from paradise into this world, and turned him back to the earth from which he was taken, dispensing to him the salvation by rebirth which is in your Christ. For you did not turn away finally from the creature you had made, O good one, nor forget the works of your hands, but you visited him in many ways through the bowels of your mercy. You sent forth prophets; you performed works of power through your saints who were well-pleasing to you in every generation; you spoke to us through the mouth of your servants the prophets, foretelling to us the salvation that should come; you gave the Law for our help; you set angels as guards over us.

But when the fullness of the times had come, you spoke to us in your Son himself, through whom also you made the ages, who, being the reflection of your glory and the impress of your substance, and bearing all things by the word of his power, thought it not robbery to be equal with you, the God and Father, but, being God before the ages, he was

seen on earth and lived among men; he was made flesh from the holy
Virgin and humbled himself, taking the form of a slave; he was con-
formed to the body of our humiliation that he might conform us to the
image of his glory. For since through man sin had entered into the
world, and through sin death, your only-begotten Son, who is in your
bosom, O God and Father, being born of a woman, the holy Mother
of God and ever-virgin Mary, born under the law, was pleased to
condemn sin in his flesh, that those who died in Adam should be made
alive in him, your Christ. And having become a citizen of this world,
he gave us commandments of salvation, turned us away from the error
of the idols, and brought us to the knowledge of you, the true God
and Father; he gained us for himself, a peculiar people, a royal priesthood, a holy nation; and when he had cleansed us with water and
sanctified us by the Holy Spirit, he gave himself as a ransom to death,
by which we were held, having been sold under sin. By means of the
cross he descended into hell, that he might fill all things with himself,
and loosed the pains of death; he rose again on the third day, making a
way to resurrection from the dead for all flesh, because it was not
possible for the prince of life to be conquered by corruption, and became the firstfruits of those who had fallen asleep, the firstborn from
the dead, so that he might be first in all ways among all things. And
ascending into the heavens, he sat down at the right hand of the[2]
majesty in the highest, and will also come to reward each man according to his works. And he left us memorials of his saving passion, these
things which we have set forth[3] according to his commandments.

For when he was about to go out to his voluntary and laudable and
life-giving death, in the night in which he gave himself up for the life
of the world, he took bread in his holy and undefiled hands and showed
it to you, the God and Father, gave thanks, blessed, sanctified, and
broke it, and gave it to his holy disciples and apostles, saying, 'Take, eat;
this is my body, which is broken for you for the forgiveness of sins.'
*People:* Amen.

Likewise also he took the cup of the fruit of the vine and mixed it,
gave thanks, blessed, sanctified, and gave it to his holy disciples and
apostles, saying, 'Drink from this, all of you; this is my blood, which
is shed for you and for many for the forgiveness of sins. Do this for my

2. *Now* your.       3. The Barberini MS breaks off here.

remembrance. For as often as you eat this bread and drink this cup, you proclaim my death, you confess my resurrection.'

Therefore, Master, we also, remembering his saving passion, his life-giving cross, his three-day burial, his resurrection from the dead, his ascension into heaven, his session at your right hand, God and Father, and his glorious and fearful second coming; (*aloud*) offer[-ing] you your own from your own, in all and through all,

*People*: we hymn you, ⟨we bless you, we give you thanks, O Lord, and pray to you, our God.⟩

Therefore, Master all-holy, we also, your sinful and unworthy servants, who have been held worthy to minister at your holy altar, not for our righteousness, for we have done nothing good upon earth, but for your mercies and compassions which you have poured out richly upon us, with confidence approach your holy altar. And having set forth the likenesses of the holy body and blood of your Christ, we pray and beseech you, O holy of holies, in the good pleasure of your bounty, that your [all-]holy Spirit may come upon us and upon these gifts set forth, and bless them and sanctify and make[4] (*he makes the sign of the cross three times, saying:*) this bread the precious body of our Lord and God and Saviour Jesus Christ. Amen. And this cup the precious blood of our Lord and God and Saviour Jesus Christ, [Amen.] which is shed for the life of the world ⟨and salvation⟩ Amen ⟨*thrice*⟩.

(*Prayer*) Unite with one another all of us who partake of the one bread and the cup into the fellowship of the one Holy Spirit; and make none of us to partake of the holy body and blood of your Christ for judgment or for condemnation, but that we may find mercy and grace with all the saints who have been well-pleasing to you from of old, forefathers, fathers, patriarchs, prophets, apostles, preachers, evangelists, martyrs, confessors, teachers, and every righteous spirit perfected in faith; (*aloud*) especially our all-holy, immaculate, highly blessed ⟨glorious⟩ Lady, Mother of God and ever-virgin Mary; (*while the diptychs are read by the deacon, the priest says the prayer:*) saint John the ⟨prophet⟩ forerunner and Baptist, ⟨the holy and honoured apostles,⟩ this saint *N.* whose memorial we are keeping, and all your saints: at their entreaties, visit us, O God.

And remember all those who have fallen asleep in hope of resurrec-

4. Greek: *anadeixai.*

tion to eternal life, and grant them rest where the light of your countenance looks upon them.

Again we pray you, Lord, remember your holy, catholic, and apostolic Church from one end of the world to the other, and grant it the peace which you purchased by the precious blood of your Christ, and stablish this holy house until the consummation of the age.

Remember, Lord, those who presented these gifts, and those for whom, and through whom, and on account of whom they presented them.

Remember, Lord, those who bring forth fruit and do good work in your holy churches and remember the poor. Reward them with rich and heavenly gifts. Grant them heavenly things for earthly, eternal things for temporal, incorruptible things for corruptible.

Remember, Lord, those in deserts and mountains and in dens and in caves of the earth.

Remember, Lord, those who live in virginity and piety ⟨and self-discipline⟩ and an honest life.

Remember, Lord, our most religious and faithful Emperor, whom you thought fit to rule the land: crown him with the weapon of truth, with the weapon of your good pleasure; overshadow his head in the day of war; strengthen his arm, exalt his right hand; make his empire mighty; subject to him all the barbarous people that delight in war; grant him [5]help and peace[5] that cannot be taken away; speak good things to his heart for your Church and all your people, that in his peace we may lead a quiet and peaceful life in all godliness and honesty.

Remember, Lord, all rule and authority, our brothers at court and all the army; preserve the good in their goodness, make the wicked good in your bounty.

Remember, Lord, the people who stand around and those who for good reason have been left, and have mercy on them and us according to the abundance of your mercy. Fill their storehouses with all good things, preserve their marriages in peace and concord; nourish the infants, instruct the youth, strengthen the old; comfort the faint-hearted, gather the scattered, bring back the wanderers and join them to your holy, catholic, and apostolic Church; set free those who are troubled by unclean spirits; sail with those that sail, journey with those

5. *Now* deep peace.

that journey; defend the widows, protect the orphans, rescue the captives, heal the sick. Be mindful, O God, of those who face trial, those in the mines, in exile, in bitter slavery, in all tribulation, necessity, and affliction, all who need your great compassion, those who love us, those who hate us, and those who commanded us, though unworthy, to pray for them.

Remember all your people, O Lord our God, and pour out upon all your rich mercy, granting to all their petitions for salvation. Be mindful of those whom we have not mentioned through ignorance or forgetfulness or the number of the names; O God, you know the age and the title of each, you know every man from his mother's womb. For you, Lord, are the help of the helpless, the hope of the hopeless, the saviour of the tempest-tossed, the haven of sailors, the physician of the sick: be all things to all men, you who know every man and his petition, his house and his need.

Rescue, Lord, this flock,[6] and every city and country, from famine, plague, earthquake, flood, fire, the sword, invasion by foreigners, and civil war.

Above all, remember, Lord, our [7]father and bishop[7] N.: grant him to your holy churches in peace, safety, honour and length of days, rightly dividing the word of your truth.

*The diptychs of the living are read.*

Remember, Lord, all the orthodox episcopate who rightly divide[8] the word of your truth; *Deacon:* N. the all-holiest metropolitan (or bishop), and him who presents these holy gifts . . . and all men and women. *People:* And all men and women.

Remember, Lord, also my unworthiness, according to the multitude of your mercies: forgive me every offence, willing and unwilling; and do not keep back the grace of your Holy Spirit from the gifts set forth, on account of my sins.

Remember, Lord, the priesthood, the diaconate in Christ, and every order of the clergy, and do not put to shame any of us who stand round your holy altar.

Look upon us, Lord, in your goodness; appear to us in your generous pity; grant us temperate and favourable weather; give kindly showers

6. *Now* city or this dwelling.    7. *Now* archbishop.    8. The Barberini MS resumes here.

to the land for bearing fruit; bless the crown of the year of your good-ness, Lord. End the divisions of the churches; quench the ragings of the nations; quickly destroy the uprising of heresies by the power of your Holy Spirit. Receive us all into your kingdom as sons of light and sons of the day; show us your peace and grant us your love, Lord our God, for you have given us all things;

(*aloud*) and grant us with one mouth and one heart to glorify and hymn your all-honourable and magnificent name, the Father and the Son and the Holy Spirit, now and always and to the ages of ages. *People:* Amen.


PRAYER AND LORD'S PRAYER
PRAYER OF INCLINATION

PRAYER OF ELEVATION
*The priest raises the holy bread and says:* The holy things for the holy people.
*People:* One is holy, one is Lord, Jesus Christ, to the glory of God the Father.


COMMUNION
THANKSGIVING FOR COMMUNION
DISMISSAL (PRAYER BEHIND THE AMBO)

# 17

# The Gallican Liturgy

The name 'Gallican' is given to a large group of rites which were used in northern Europe until they were superseded by the Roman rite in the eighth century. They have features in common with the Ambrosian rite used at Milan and with Eastern liturgies. In Gallican masses the place of the canon is taken by a set of variable prayers arranged around the Sanctus and the Institution Narrative. The prayers are often addressed to Christ rather than to the Father, and sometimes lack any anamnesis. They are written in a florid style quite unlike the Roman, and often at considerable length. The present set is for any Sunday.

BIBLIOGRAPHY
*Prex Eucharistica*, pp. 467–8 (bibliography, p. 462).
W. S. Porter, *The Gallican Rite* (1958).
Bouyer, pp. 315–37.

SALUTATION
PROPHETIA (BENEDICTUS)
COLLECT POST PROPHETIAM
OLD TESTAMENT LESSON AND EPISTLE
BENEDICITE
GOSPEL
SERMON
DISMISSAL OF CATECHUMENS AND PENITENTS
PRAYERS OF THE FAITHFUL
OFFERTORY
PRAEFATIO (ADMONITION TO EARNEST PRAYER)
COLLECTIO (PRAYER FOR ACCEPTANCE OF PRAYERS)
NAMES AND PRAYER POST NOMINA (OFFERTORY PRAYER)
PRAYER AD PACEM AND KISS OF PEACE

SURSUM CORDA

### CONTESTATIO OR IMMOLATIO (PREFACE)

*Priest:* It is fitting and right, right and just, here and everywhere to give you thanks, Lord, holy Father, eternal God; you snatched us from perpetual death and the last darkness of hell, and gave mortal matter, put together from the liquid mud, to your Son and to eternity. Who is acceptable to tell your praises, who can make a full declaration of your works? Every tongue marvels at you, all priests extol your glory.

When you had overcome chaos and the confusion of the beginning and the darkness in which things swam, you gave wonderful forms to the amazed elements: the tender world blushed at the fires of the sun, and the rude earth wondered at the dealings of the moon. And lest no inhabitant should adorn the world, and the sun's orb shine on emptiness, your hands made from clay a more excellent likeness, which a holy fire quickened within, and a lively soul brought to life throughout its idle parts. We may not look, Father, into the inner mysteries. To you alone is known the majesty of your work: what there is in man, that the blood held in the veins washes the fearful limbs and the living earth; that the loose appearances of bodies are held together by tightening nerves, and the individual bones gain strength from the organs within them.

But whence comes so great a bounty to miserable men, that we should be formed in the likeness of you and your Son, that an earthly thing should be eternal? We abandoned the commandments of your blessed majesty; we were plunged, mortal once more, into the earth from which we came, and mourned the loss of the eternal comfort of your gift. But your manifold goodness and inestimable majesty sent the Word of salvation from heaven, that he should be made flesh by taking a human body, and should care for that which the age had lost and the ancient wounds. Therefore all the angels, with the manifold multitude of the saints, praise him with unceasing voice, saying:

### SANCTUS

*People:* Holy, holy, holy, Lord God of Sabaoth; heaven and earth are full of your glory. Hosanna in the highest. Blessed is he who comes in the name of the Lord. Hosanna in the highest.

## POST SANCTUS

*Priest:* As the supernal creatures resound on high the praise of your glory, your goodness wished that it should be known also to your servants; and this proclamation, made in the starry realms, was revealed to your servants by the gift of your magnificence, not only to be known but also to be imitated.

## SECRETA (INSTITUTION NARRATIVE)

(*privately*) Who, the day before he suffered for the salvation of us all, standing in the midst of his disciples and apostles, took bread in his holy hands, looked up to heaven to you, God the Father almighty, gave thanks, blessed, and broke it, and gave it to his disciples, saying, 'Take, eat from this, all of you; for this is my body, which shall be broken for the life of the age.' Likewise after supper he took the cup in his hands, looked up to heaven to you, God the Father almighty, gave thanks, blessed it, and handed it to his apostles, saying, 'Take, drink from this, all of you; for this is the cup of my holy blood, of the new and eternal covenant, which is shed for you and for many for the forgiveness of sins.' In addition to these words he said to them, 'As often as you eat from this bread and drink from this cup, you will do it for my remembrance, showing my passion to all, (and) you will look for my coming until I come (again).'

## POST SECRETA or POST MYSTERIUM

(*aloud*) Therefore, most merciful Father, look upon the commandments of your Son, the mysteries of the Church, (your) gifts to those who believe: they are offered by suppliants, and for suppliants they are to be sought;

through Jesus Christ your Son, our God and Lord and Saviour, who, with you, Lord, and the Holy Spirit, reigns for ever, eternal Godhead, to the ages of ages.

*People:* Amen.

FRACTION
LORD'S PRAYER
BLESSING

**COMMUNION**
**THANKSGIVING FOR COMMUNION**
**COLLECT AND DISMISSAL**

# 18

# The Mozarabic Liturgy

A liturgy of the Gallican type (see p. 91) was developed in Spain under the Visigoths and survived much later than the Gallican rite, owing to the Moorish occupation, which gave rise to the name 'Mozarabic'. The text translated below is for daily use. The translation of another text may be found in C. Vagaggini, *The Canon of the Mass and Liturgical Reform* 1967, pp. 41-9.

BIBLIOGRAPHY
*Prex Eucharistica*, pp. 497-8 (bibliography p. 495).
W. S. Porter, *The Gallican Rite* (1958).
Bouyer, pp. 315-37.

INTROIT
SALUTATION
GLORIA IN EXCELSIS
COLLECT POST GLORIAM
OLD TESTAMENT LESSON
BENEDICITE
EPISTLE
PSALM
GOSPEL
SERMON
DISMISSAL OF CATECHUMENS AND PENITENTS
OFFERTORY
MISSA (ADMONITION TO EARNEST PRAYER)
PRAYERS OF THE FAITHFUL
ALIA (PRAYER FOR ACCEPTANCE OF PRAYERS)
NAMES AND PRAYER POST NOMINA
PRAYER AD PACEM, THE GRACE, KISS OF PEACE, ANTIPHON AD
    PACEM

SURSUM CORDA

*Priest:*    I will go to the altar of God:
*People:*    To the God of my joy and gladness.
*Priest:*    Ears to the Lord.[1]
*People:*    We have them with the Lord.
*Priest:*    Up with your hearts.[1]
*People:*    Let us lift them to the Lord.
*Priest:*    To our God and Lord Jesus Christ, Son of God, who is in heaven, let us offer fitting praise and fitting thanks.
*People:*    It is fitting and right.

ILLATIO (PREFACE)

*Priest:* It is fitting and right, almighty Father, that we should give you thanks through your Son Jesus Christ, the true high priest for ever, the only priest without spot of sin; for by his blood, which cleanses the hearts of all, we sacrifice to you the propitiatory victim, not only for the sins of the people, but also for our offences that by the intercession of our high-priest for us, every sin committed by the weakness of the flesh may be forgiven; to him rightly all angels cry unceasingly and say,

SANCTUS

*People:* Holy, holy, holy, Lord God of Sabaoth. Heaven and earth are full of the glory of your majesty. Hosanna to the Son of David. Blessed is he who comes in the name of the Lord. Hosanna in the highest.

POST SANCTUS

*Priest:* Truly holy, truly blessed is your Son, Jesus Christ our Lord, in whose name we offer to you, Lord, these holy offerings, praying that you will be pleased to accept what we offer, and bless it by the outpouring of your Holy Spirit.

SECRETA (INSTITUTION NARRATIVE)

(*privately*) God the Lord and eternal redeemer, who, the day before he suffered, took bread, gave thanks, blessed, and broke it, and gave it to his disciples, saying, 'Take and eat; this is my body, which shall be betrayed for you. As often as you eat it, do this for my remembrance.'

1. The Latin has no verb.

Amen. Likewise the cup also, after supper, saying, 'This is the cup of the new covenant in my blood, which shall be shed for you and for many for the forgiveness of sins. As often as you drink it, do this for my remembrance.' Amen. 'As often as you eat this bread and drink this cup, you proclaim the death of the Lord, until he comes in glory from heaven.'

*People:* So we believe, Lord Jesus.

POST PRIDIE

*Priest (aloud):* Bless Lord, this victim that is offered to you in honour of your name, and sanctify the minds and purify the wills of those who partake of it. Amen.

By your gift, holy Lord, for you create, sanctify, quicken, bless, and provide for us your unworthy servants all these truly good things, that they may be blessed by you, our God, to the ages of ages.

*People:* Amen.

FRACTION
NICENE CREED
LORD'S PRAYER
BLESSING

COMMUNION

The body of our Lord Jesus Christ be your salvation.
The blood of Christ remain with you as true redemption.

ANTIPHON AND COLLECT
DISMISSAL

# 19

# Ambrose: *On the Sacraments*

The treatise *De Sacramentis*, whose authenticity was once suspect, is now generally held to contain 'the actual words of the addresses of Ambrose to the newly baptized, taken down at the time by a *notarius*'.[1] The addresses will have been delivered in Milan, where Ambrose was bishop until his death in A.D. 397. The canon from which he quotes is similar to, but significantly different from, the Roman; and the relationship between the two remains uncertain. A hypothetical reconstruction of a non-Roman canon will be found on p. 101.

BIBLIOGRAPHY

H. Chadwick, *Saint Ambrose on the Sacraments* (1960).
J. H. Srawley, ed., *Saint Ambrose on the Sacraments and on the Mysteries* (1950).
J. H. Srawley, *The Early History of the Liturgy* (1949), pp. 150–64.

*Book 4*, 13   Who therefore is the author of the sacraments, if not Jesus? Those sacraments came from heaven, for all counsel is from heaven. It was a great and divine miracle that God rained manna on the people from heaven, and the people ate it without working for it.

14   Perhaps you will say, 'My bread is common (bread).' But that bread is bread before the words of the sacraments; when consecration has been applied, from (being) bread it becomes the flesh of Christ. And by what words and whose sayings does consecration take place? The Lord Jesus's. For all the other things which are said in the earlier parts (of the service) are said by the bishop[2]: [3]praise is offered to God, prayer is made for the people[3], for kings, for others; when the time comes for the venerated sacrament to be accomplished, the bishop no longer uses his own words, but uses the words of Christ. So the word of Christ accomplishes this sacrament.

---

1. Srawley, *Early History*, p. 155.   2. Latin: *sacerdos*.
3. *Or* praise to God, prayer is offered, intercession is made for the people.

21   Do you wish to know how consecration is done with heavenly words? Hear what the words are. The bishop says:

*Make for us this offering approved, reasonable, acceptable, because it is the figure of the body and blood of our Lord Jesus Christ; who, the day before he suffered, took bread in his holy hands, looked up to heaven to you, holy Father almighty, eternal God, gave thanks, blessed, and broke it, and handed it to his apostles and disciples, saying, 'Take and eat from this, all of you; for this is my body, which will be broken for many.'*

22   Notice this. *Likewise also after supper, the day before he suffered, he took the cup, looked up to heaven to you, holy Father, almighty, eternal God, gave thanks, blessed, and handed it to his apostles and disciples, saying, 'Take and drink from this, all of you; for this is my blood.'*

See, all those words up to 'Take', whether the body or the blood, are the evangelist's; then they are Christ's words, 'Take and drink from this, all of you; for this is my blood.'

23   Notice these points. He says, 'who, the day before he suffered, took bread in his holy hands'. Before it is consecrated, it is bread; but when the words of Christ are added, it is the body of Christ. Then hear his words: 'Take and eat from this, all of you; for this is my body.' And before the words of Christ, the cup is full of wine and water; when the words of Christ have been employed, the blood is created which redeems his people. So you see in what ways the word of Christ has power to change everything. Our Lord Jesus himself bore witness that we should receive his body and blood. Ought we to doubt his faith and witness?

25   So you do not say Amen to no purpose: you confess in spirit that you are receiving the body of Christ. When you seek it, the bishop says to you, '*The body of Christ*', and you say '*Amen*', which means 'It is true'. What your tongue confesses, let your feelings retain; so that you may know that this is a sacrament, whose likeness has come first.

26   Next, you must learn how great a sacrament it is. See what he says: '*As often as you do this, so often you will make remembrance of me until I come again.*'

27   And the bishop says:

*Therefore, remembering his most glorious passion and resurrection from the dead, and ascension into heaven, we offer you this spotless victim, reasonable victim, bloodless victim, this holy bread and this cup of eternal life; and we pray and beseech you to receive this offering on your altar on high by the hands of your angels, as you vouchsafed to receive the gifts of your righteous servant Abel, and the sacrifice of our patriarch Abraham, and that which the high-priest Melchizedek offered to you.*

Book 5, 18. Now what is left but the (Lords) Prayer? . . .

Book 6, 24. . . . What follows? Hear what the bishop says:

*Through our Lord Jesus Christ, in whom and with whom honour, praise, glory, magnificence and power are yours, with the Holy Spirit, from the ages, and now, and always, and to all the ages of ages. Amen.*

# 20

# Non-Roman Versions of the Canon

Before the Roman Canon became universally accepted, there must have been many canons in use in the West, some related more or less closely to the Roman, some quite independent. Purely by chance, five of the few surviving fragments of such canons, when put together, make up a complete canon.

Fragment 1 is the second of two quoted by an anonymous Arian author, writing probably between A.D. 380 and 450 in northern Italy, who must have copied them from an orthodox sacramentary. This example is largely independent of the Roman; the *Sursum corda* is implied, but the Sanctus is absent.

Fragments 2 and 4 are taken from *post-pridie* prayers of the Mozarabic Liturgy (see p. 96). They are closely related to the Roman Canon, but retain certain features which have been discarded at Rome (their date is uncertain).

Fragments 3 and 5 come from *De Sacramentis*, the catechetical addresses of St Ambrose, delivered in Milan between A.D. 374 and 397. The canon on which Ambrose is commenting is likewise a near relation of the Roman; most probably both derive from a common ancestor. (See further pp. 98–100.)

Another reconstruction may be found in C. Vagaggini, *The Canon of the Mass and Liturgical Reform* (1967), pp. 28–34.

BIBLIOGRAPHY

1. *Prex Eucharistica*, p. 422.
Dix, *The Shape*, pp. 539–41.

2. *Prex Eucharistica*, p. 428, note 1 (*Liber Ordinum*, p. 321).
L. Eizenhöfer, *Canon Missae Romanae*, vol. 2, p. 41 (no. 179).
B. Botte & C. Mohrmann, *L'Ordinaire de la Messe*, p. 21.

3. *Prex Eucharistica*, pp. 421–2.
H. Chadwick, *St Ambrose on the Sacraments* (1960), pp. 34–6.
J. H. Srawley, *The Early History of the Liturgy* (1949), pp. 155–62.

4. *Prex Eucharistica*, p. 433, note 1 (*Liber Ordinum*, p. 265).
Eizenhöfer, vol. 2, p. 149 (no. 1020).
Botte & Mohrmann, pp. 19–20.

5. Chadwick, p. 53.

### I

It is fitting and right, it is just and right, that we should give you thanks for all things, O Lord, holy Father, almighty eternal God, for you deigned in the incomparable splendour of your goodness that light should shine in darkness, by sending us Jesus Christ as saviour of our souls. For our salvation he humbled himself and subjected himself even unto death that, when we had been restored to that immortality which Adam lost, he might make us heirs and sons to himself.

Neither can we be sufficient to give thanks to your great generosity for this loving kindness with any praises; but we ask (you) of your great and merciful goodness to hold accepted this sacrifice which we offer to you, standing before the face of your divine goodness; through Jesus Christ our Lord and God, through whom we ask and beseech . . .

### 2

Through him we pray and beseech you, almighty Father, vouchsafe to accept and bless these offerings and these unblemished sacrifices which we offer to you above all for your holy Catholic Church: vouchsafe to grant it peace; it is spread through the whole world in your peace.

Remember, Lord, also, we pray, your servants who in honour of your Saints NN. pay their vows to the living and true God, for the forgiveness of all their sins. Vouchsafe to make their offering blessed, ratified, and reasonable; it is the image and likeness of the body and blood of Jesus Christ, your Son and our Redeemer.

### 3

. . . Make for us this offering approved, reasonable, acceptable, because it is the figure of the body and blood of our Lord Jesus Christ; who, the day before he suffered, took bread in his holy hands, looked up to heaven to you, holy Father, almighty, eternal God, gave thanks, blessed and broke it, and handed it to his apostles and disciples, saying, 'Take and eat from this, all of you, for this is my body, which will be broken for many.' Likewise also after supper, the day before he suffered, he took the cup, looked up to heaven to you, holy Father, almighty, eternal God, and gave thanks, blessed, and handed it to his apostles and disciples, saying, 'Take and drink from this, all of you, for this is my blood. As often as you do this, so often you will make remembrance of me until I come again.'

Therefore, remembering his most glorious passion, and resurrection from the dead, and ascension into heaven, we offer you this spotless victim, reasonable victim, bloodless victim, this holy bread and cup of eternal life: and we pray and beseech you (to) receive this offering on your altar on high by the hands of your angels, as you vouchsafed to receive the gifts of your righteous servant Abel, and the sacrifice of our patriarch Abraham, and that which the high-priest Melchizedek offered to you.

### 4

We beseech and entreat you to accept and bless this offering also, as you accepted the gifts of your righteous servant Abel, and the sacrifice of the patriarch Abraham our father, and that which your high-priest Melchizedek offered to you. Let your blessing, I pray, descend here invisibly, as once it used to descend on the victims of the fathers. Let a sweet-smelling savour ascend to the sight of your divine majesty by the hands of your angel. And let your Holy Spirit be borne down upon those solemn things, to sanctify both the offerings and the prayers alike of the people who stand here and offer, that all who taste of this body may receive healing for our souls.

### 5

Through our Lord Jesus Christ, in whom and with whom honour, praise, glory, magnificence and power are yours, with the Holy Spirit, from the ages, and now, and always, and to all the ages of ages. Amen.

# 21

# The Mass of the Roman Rite

The Roman Canon cannot be dated with precision. Quotations and parallels begin to appear towards the end of the fourth century in such writers as Ambrose and Ambrosiaster, and in the letter of Pope Innocent I to Bishop Decentius (A.D. 416). The text translated below is based on the oldest manuscripts, none older than the eighth century. It differs from the standard text of 1571 chiefly in the absence of the phrases printed below in angle-brackets. 1571 also inserts 'and' at several points, and adds 'the same' and 'Amen' to the phrases 'through Christ our Lord'.

A selection is included of the priest's private prayers from the 1571 text, all later than 800; further medieval examples may be found in the Sarum Missal.[1]

The literature is enormous, and the following bibliography is only a starting-point.

BIBLIOGRAPHY

*Prex Eucharistica*, pp. 424–6 (with bibliography).

B. Botte, *Le canon de la messe romaine* (1935, reprinted 1962).

B. Botte & C. Mohrmann, *L'Ordinaire de la messe* (1953).

L. Eizenhöfer, *Canon Missae Romanae* (I, 1954; II, 1966).

J. A. Jungmann, *The Mass of the Roman Rite* (2 vols., 1951) (1 vol. edition 1959).

Dix, *The Shape* (1945), pp. 434–612.

G. G. Willis, *Essays in Early Roman Liturgy* (1964).
   *Further Essays in Early Roman Liturgy* (1968).

C. Vagaggini, *The Canon of the Mass and Liturgical Reform* (1967).

Bouyer, pp. 227–43.

PSALM 43

CONFESSION AND ABSOLUTION

INTROIT PSALM

KYRIES

1. G. J. Cuming, *A History of Anglican Liturgy* (1969), pp. 287–9.

GLORIA IN EXCELSIS
COLLECT OF THE DAY
EPISTLE
GRADUAL AND SEQUENCE
GOSPEL
SERMON
NICENE CREED
OFFERTORY

OFFERTORY PRAYERS

Receive, holy Father, almighty, eternal God, this unblemished offering which I, your unworthy servant, present to you, my living and true God, for my innumerable sins, offences, and negligences; for all who stand round, and for all faithful Christians, alive and dead; that it may avail for my salvation and theirs to eternal life.

O God, who in a wonderful way created human nature in its dignity, and more wonderfully restored it; grant us through the mystery of this water and wine, to share his divinity who vouchsafed to share our humanity, Jesus Christ, your Son, our Lord; who is alive and reigns with you as God in the unity of the Holy Spirit through all the ages of ages.

We offer you, Lord, the cup of salvation, and pray that of your kindness it may ascend in the sight of your divine majesty for our salvation and that of the whole world, in a sweet-smelling savour.

Receive, Lord, our humble spirits and contrite hearts; and may our sacrifice be performed today in your sight so as to please you, Lord God.

Come, Sanctifier, almighty, eternal God, and bless this sacrifice prepared for your holy name.

Through the intercession of blessed Michael the archangel, who stands at the right of the altar of incense, and of all the elect, may the Lord vouchsafe to bless this incense and receive it as a sweet-smelling savour; through Christ our Lord.

(Psalm 141.2–4; Psalm 25.6–12)

Receive, holy Trinity, this offering which we offer you in memory of the passion, resurrection, and ascension of our Lord Jesus Christ; and in honour of the blessed ever-virgin Mary, and blessed John the

Baptist, and the holy apostles Peter and Paul, and of . . . and all saints; that it may avail to their honour and our salvation. May they vouchsafe to intercede for us in heaven, whose memory we celebrate on earth, through the same Jesus Christ our Lord.

Pray, brothers, that my sacrifice and yours may be acceptable to God, the almighty Father.

*People:* May God receive the sacrifice from your hands to the praise and glory of his name, and to our benefit, and that of all his holy Church.

THE CANON

*Priest:*    The Lord be with you.
*People:*   And with your spirit.
*Priest:*    Up with your hearts.[2]
*People:*   We have them with the Lord.
*Priest:*    Let us give thanks to the Lord our God.
*People:*   It is fitting and right.

*Priest:* It is fitting and right, our duty and our salvation, that we should always and everywhere give you thanks, O Lord, holy Father, almighty eternal God, through Christ our Lord; [3]through whom angels praise, dominions adore, powers fear, the heavens and the heavenly hosts and the blessed seraphim, joining together in exultation celebrate your majesty.[3]

We pray you, bid our voices to be admitted with theirs, beseeching you, confessing you, and saying:

*People:* Holy, holy, holy, Lord God of Sabaoth. Heaven and earth are full of your glory. Hosanna in the highest. Blessed is he who comes in the name of the Lord. Hosanna in the highest.

*Priest:* We therefore pray and beseech you, most merciful Father, through your Son Jesus Christ our Lord, to accept and bless these gifts, these offerings, these holy and unblemished sacrifices; above all, those which we offer to you for your holy catholic Church: vouchsafe to grant it peace, protection, unity, and guidance throughout the world, together with your servant *N.* our pope, and *N.* our bishop, and all orthodox upholders of the catholic and apostolic faith.

Remember, Lord, your servants, men and women, and all who stand

2. The Latin has no verb.        3. The Preface varies according to the occasion.

around (us), whose faith and devotion are known to you, for whom we offer to you or who offer to you this sacrifice of praise for themselves and for their own, for the redemption of their souls, for the hope of their salvation and safety, and pay their vows to you, the living, true and eternal God.

In fellowship with, (*here a seasonal clause may follow*) and venerating the memory above all of the glorious ever-virgin Mary, Mother of our God and Lord Jesus Christ, and also of your blessed apostles and martyrs Peter, Paul, Andrew, James, John, Thomas, James, Philip, Bartholomew, Matthew, Simon and Thaddaeus, Linus, Cletus, Clement, Xystus, Cornelius, Cyprian, Laurence, Chrysogonus, John and Paul, Cosmas and Damian, and all your saints, by whose merits and prayers grant us to be defended in all things by the help of your protection; through Christ our Lord.

[4]Therefore, Lord, we pray you graciously to accept this offering made by us, your servants, and also by your whole family; and to order our days in peace; and to command that we are snatched from eternal damnation and numbered among the flock of your elect; through Christ our Lord.[4]

Vouchsafe, we beseech you, O God, to make this offering wholly blessed, approved, ratified, reasonable, and acceptable; that it may become to us the body and blood of your dearly beloved Son Jesus Christ our Lord;

who, on the day before he suffered, took bread in his holy and reverend hands, lifted up his eyes to heaven to you, his almighty God and Father, gave thanks to you, blessed, broke, and gave it to his disciples, saying, 'Take and eat from this, all of you; for this is my body.' Likewise after supper, taking also this glorious cup in his holy and reverend hands, again he gave thanks to you, blessed, and gave it to his disciples, saying, 'Take and drink from it, all of you; for this is the cup of my blood, of the new and eternal covenant, the mystery of faith, which will be shed for you and for many for forgiveness of sins. As often as you do this, you will do it for my remembrance.'

Therefore also, Lord, we your servants, and also your holy people, have in remembrance the blessed passion of your Son Christ our Lord, likewise his resurrection from the dead, and also his glorious ascension

4. This paragraph varies according to the occasion.

into heaven; we offer to your excellent majesty from your gifts and bounty a pure victim, a holy victim, an unspotted victim, the holy bread of eternal life and the cup of everlasting salvation.

Vouchsafe to look upon them with a favourable and kindly countenance, and accept them as you vouchsafed to accept the gifts of your righteous servant Abel, and the sacrifice of our patriarch Abraham, and that which your high-priest Melchizedek offered to you, a holy sacrifice, an unblemished victim.

We humbly beseech you, almighty God, to bid them be borne by the hands of your angel to your altar on high, in the sight of your divine majesty, that all of us who have received the most holy body and blood of your Son by partaking at this altar may be filled with all heavenly blessing and grace; through Christ our Lord.

Remember also, Lord, the names of those who have gone before us with the sign of faith, and sleep in the sleep of peace. We beseech you to grant to them and to all who rest in Christ a place of restoration, light, and peace; through Christ our Lord.

To us sinners your servants also, who trust in the multitude of your mercies, vouchsafe to grant some part and fellowship with your holy apostles and martyrs, with John, Stephen, Matthias, Barnabas, Ignatius, Alexander, Marcellinus, Peter, Felicity, Perpetua, Agatha, Lucy, Agnes, Cecilia, Anastasia, and with all your saints: into whose company we ask that you will admit us, not weighing our merit, but bounteously forgiving through Christ our Lord.[5]

Through him, Lord, you ever create, sanctify, quicken, bless and bestow all these good things on us. Through him and with him and in him all honour and glory is yours, O God the Father almighty, in the unity of the Holy Spirit, through all the ages of ages. Amen.

SELECTED BLESSINGS
The blessings which follow, to be inserted before the doxology above, are taken from the Gregorian ('Hadrianum') and Leonine ('Veronense') Sacramentaries respectively. They have obvious affinities with those in the *Apostolic Tradition* (p. 23).

5. Here a blessing may follow.

*Blessing of chrism on Maundy Thursday*
Send forth, Lord, your Holy Spirit the Paraclete from heaven on this
richness of the olive, which you vouchsafed to bring forth from the
green tree for the healing of the body; that by your holy blessing it may
be to all who anoint and touch a protection to mind and body, to drive
out all ills and all infirmities, all sickness of body; your perfect chrism,
with which you anointed priests, kings, prophets, and martyrs, blessed
by you, Lord, remaining in our reins, in the name of Jesus Christ our
Lord; through him, Lord, you ever create . . . (*as above*).

*Blessing of water and milk and honey at Pentecost*
Bless, Lord, also these your creatures of water, honey, and milk; and
give your servants to drink from this fountain of the water of eternal
life, which is the Spirit of truth, and nourish them with this milk and
honey, as you promised to our fathers, Abraham, Isaac, and Jacob, to
bring them into the Promised Land, a land flowing with milk and
honey. Unite your servants therefore, Lord, to the Holy Spirit, as this
milk and honey was united, thereby signifying the union of heavenly
and earthly substance in Christ Jesus our Lord. Through him, Lord, you
ever create . . . (*as above*)

LORD'S PRAYER, WITH EMBOLISM AND FRACTION
KISS OF PEACE

COMMUNION PRAYERS
May this sacramental mixing of the body and blood of our Lord Jesus
Christ bring us who receive it to eternal life.
    Lamb of God, you take away the sins of the world: have mercy on us.
    Lamb of God, you take away the sins of the world: have mercy on us.
    Lamb of God, you take away the sins of the world: grant us peace.
    Lord Jesus Christ, Son of the living God, who by the Father's will
and the Holy Spirit's help, gave life to the world through your death:
by this your holy body and blood, free me from all my wickedness and
every evil; make me always to cleave to your commandments, and
never let me be separated from you; for you are alive and reign as God
with the same God the Father and the Holy Spirit, to the ages of ages.

May the receiving of your body, Lord Jesus Christ, which in my unworthiness I dare to take, bring on me neither judgment nor condemnation; but in your mercy may it be to me protection of mind and body, and receiving of a remedy; for you are alive and reign as God with God the Father, in the unity of the Holy Spirit for all the ages of ages.

COMMUNION

The body of our Lord Jesus Christ keep your soul in eternal life.
The blood of our Lord Jesus Christ keep your soul in eternal life.

POST COMMUNION PRAYERS
DISMISSAL

# 22

# *Ordo Romanus Primus*

This document describes the ceremonial used when the pope visited one of the churches in Rome for a stational Mass. Internal evidence suggests that it was compiled about A.D. 700 by someone with an intimate knowledge of the organization of the papal court. As such, it may be regarded as thoroughly reliable. The text translated below is that of the oldest manuscript, Saint-Gall 614, written about A.D. 850. Later manuscripts make numerous additions to the text, which reveal minor developments of the ceremonial.

BIBLIOGRAPHY

M. Andrieu, *Les Ordines Romani du Haut Moyen Age*, vol. 2 (1948), pp. 74–108.

E. G. C. F. Atchley, *Ordo Romanus Primus* (1905) (with full commentary).

J. A. Jungmann, *The Mass of the Roman Rite* (1 vol. edition) (1959), pp. 49–56.

PRELIMINARIES TO THE SERVICE

INTROIT

KYRIES

GLORIA IN EXCELSIS

COLLECT

EPISTLE

GRADUAL AND ALLELUIA

GOSPEL

SALUTATION AND OREMUS (BUT NO PRAYER)

Then as the deacon goes to the altar, an acolyte comes with a chalice and a corporal over (it), raises the chalice in his left hand and hands the corporal to the deacon. He takes it off the chalice and lays it on the right side of the altar, throwing the other end to the second deacon so that they can spread it out.

A subdeacon with the empty chalice follows the archdeacon.

The pope, after saying *Let us pray*, goes down at once to the senatorial area, the chancellor holding his right hand and the chief counsellor his left, and receives the offerings of the princes in the order of their authorities. After him the archdeacon receives the flasks and pours them into a larger chalice held by a district subdeacon. He is followed by an acolyte with a bowl outside his cope into which the chalice is poured out when it is full. The district subdeacon receives the offerings from the pope and hands them to the subdeacon in attendance, and he puts them in a linen cloth held by two acolytes. After the pope, a hebdomadary bishop receives the rest of the offerings, so that he may put them with his own hand in the linen cloth which follows him. After him the deacon who follows the archdeacon receives (the flasks) and pours them into the bowl with his own hand.

The pope, before crossing to the women's side, goes down before the *confessio* and receives the offerings of the chancellor, the secretary, and the chief counsellor; for on festivals they offer at the altar after the deacons. Likewise the pope goes up to the women's side and carries out the above order. Likewise the presbyters do also, if need be, after him or in the presbytery.

After this the pope, with the chancellor and the secretary holding his hands, returns to his seat and washes his hands. The archdeacon, standing before the altar, when the collection is completed, washes his hands; then he looks towards the pope, who nods to him; and thus saluted he goes to the altar.

Then the district subdeacons, taking the offerings from the subdeacon in attendance, hand them to the archdeacon, and he arranges them on the altar; the subdeacons hand them on each side. The altar being prepared, the archdeacon takes a flask from the oblationary subdeacon and pours it through a strainer into the chalice, and then the deacons' (flasks). Then the subdeacon in attendance goes down to the choir, takes a ewer from the chief singer and brings it to the archdeacon, who pours it into the chalice, making the sign of the cross. Then the deacons go up to the pope. When they see them, the chancellor, the secretary, and the chief district counsellor and the district notaries and the district counsellors come down from their ranks to stand in their proper places.

Then the pope rises from his seat, goes down to the altar, salutes it, and receives the offerings from the hebdomadary presbyter and the deacons. Then the archdeacon receives the pope's offerings from the oblationary and gives them to the pope. When the pope has placed them on the altar, the archdeacon takes the chalice from the district subdeacon and puts it on the altar near the pope's offering with the offertory-veil twisted round its handles. He lays the veil on the corner of the altar, and stands behind the pope. The pope, bowing slightly to the altar, looks at the choir and nods to them to be silent.

The offertory finished, the bishops are standing behind the pope, the senior in the middle, then in order; and the archdeacon on the right of the bishops, the second deacon on the left, and the others in order arranged in a line. And the district subdeacons go behind the altar when the offertory is finished, and look at the pope, so that, when he says *For ever and ever* or *The Lord be with you* or *Lift up your hearts* or *Let us give thanks*, they may be ready to answer, standing upright until they begin to say the angelic hymn, that is *Holy, holy, holy*.

And when they have finished, the pope alone rises for the canon, but the bishops, priests, deacons, and subdeacons remain bowed. And when he has said *To us sinners also*, the subdeacons rise; when he has said *Through whom all these things, O Lord*, the archdeacon rises alone; when he has said *Through him and with him*, (the archdeacon) lifts up the chalice by the handles with the offertory-veil and holds it, raising it towards the pope. The pope touches the side of the chalice with the offerings, saying *Through him and with him* up to *For all the ages of ages*, and puts the offerings in their place, and the archdeacon puts the chalice near them.

We have left out something about the paten: when (the pope) begins the canon, an acolyte comes to his side with a linen cloth tied round his neck and holds the paten before his breast on the right side until the middle of the canon. Then the subdeacon in attendance receives it outside his chasuble and comes before the altar, and waits for a district subdeacon to receive it.

When the canon is finished, the district subdeacon stands with the paten behind the archdeacon. When he has said *and safe from all distress*, the archdeacon turns, kisses the paten, and gives it to the second deacon to hold. When he has said *The peace of the Lord be always with you*, he makes the sign of the cross over the chalice with his hand three times, (and puts a consecrated fragment into it). The archdeacon gives the peace to the chief bishop, then the rest in order and the people likewise.

Then the pope breaks the offering on the right and leaves the fragment which he has broken off on the altar; but he puts his other offerings on the paten which a deacon is holding. Then at once he goes up to his seat.

The archdeacon takes the chalice from above the altar, gives it to a district subdeacon, and he holds it near the right corner of the altar until the offerings are broken. The subdeacons in attendance with the acolytes, who carry little bags, come on the right and on the left; the acolytes hold out their arms with the little bags, and the subdeacons in attendance stand at each corner of the altar. They make ready the openings of the little bags for the archdeacon to put the offerings in them, first on the right, then on the left. Then the acolytes go to the right and left through the bishops round the altar; the rest go down to the presbyters, for them to break the hosts. Two district subdeacons proceed to the seat, carrying the paten to the deacons, for the fraction. They look at the pope, so that he may nod to them to do the fraction; and when he nods to them, they return the pope's salutation and do the fraction.

When the altar has been cleared of the offerings, except for the fragment which the pope broke off his own offering and left on the altar (they do it thus so that the altar should not be without the sacrifice while the solemnities of mass are celebrated), the archdeacon looks at the choir and nods to them to say *O Lamb of God*, and goes to the paten with the rest.

When the fraction has been completed, the second deacon takes the paten from the subdeacon and takes it to the seat, in order that the pope may communicate. When he has communicated, he makes the sign of the cross three times over the fragment from which he has bitten, and puts it in the chalice in the hands of the archdeacon. And he is communicated thus by the archdeacon.

Then the archdeacon comes with the chalice to the corner of the altar, and announces the (next) station. When he has poured a little from the chalice into the bowl held by an acolyte, the bishops come up first to the seat, that they may communicate from the hand of the pope in order. The presbyters also come up to communicate. The chief bishop receives the chalice from the archdeacon, and stands at the corner of the altar; he communicates the remaining ranks down to the chief counsellor. Then the archdeacon receives the chalice from him, and pours it into the above-mentioned bowl, and hands the chalice to a district subdeacon, who gives him the reed with which he communicates the people. The subdeacon in attendance receives the chalice and gives it to an acolyte, by whom it is replaced in the sacristy.

When (the archdeacon) has administered to those whom the pope communicated, the pope comes down from his seat with the chancellor and the chief counsellor, to administer to those who are in the senatorial area, after which the archdeacon communicates them. After the archdeacon the bishops give the communion, the deacons administering after them. For (when) the pope came to give the communion, an acolyte went before him with a linen cloth hanging round his neck, with which he held the paten with the host. Likewise they go after the deacons also with ewers and bowls, pouring the wine into gemellions for the communion to the people. When they do this, they cross from right to left. When the chancellor nods, the presbyters, by command of the pope, communicate the people in both kinds.

Now as soon as the pope begins to give the communion in the senatorial area, the choir at once begin the communion antiphon by turns with the subdeacons, and sing until all the people have been communicated, and the pope nods for them to say *Glory be to the Father*; and then, when they have repeated the verse, they fall silent.

The pope, as soon as he has communicated those on the women's side, returns to his seat and communicates the district officials in order as they stand in line. When the station has been announced, they go up to the altar. The archdeacon gives them the communion after the pope. When all have communicated, the pope sits down and washes his hands.

COLLECT
DISMISSAL
BLESSING

## 23

# Zwingli: a. *Epicheiresis* 1523 and
# b. *Action oder Bruch* 1525

Zwingli's first liturgical work appeared in the pamphlet *De Canone Missae Epicheiresis* (*An Attack upon the Canon of the Mass*) in 1523. It was written in Latin and, despite its title, contained his proposals for the revision of the whole of the Roman rite. While he was prepared to retain most of the liturgy of the word, he replaced the canon after the Sanctus and Preface with four prayers of his own composition. His *Action oder Bruch des Nachtmals* (*Action or Use of the Lord's Supper*) published two years later was much more radical and, apart from the Institution Narrative, the canon had disappeared completely. This became the norm for all later Zwinglian rites. The translations here are from the texts provided in Bretschneider's *Corpus Reformatorum*, vols. 39 and 40.

BIBLIOGRAPHY

W. D. Maxwell, *An Outline of Christian Worship* (1945), pp. 81-7.
Y. Brilioth, *Eucharistic Faith and Practice Evangelical and Catholic* (1930), pp. 153-164.
A. Barclay, *The Protestant Doctrine of the Lord's Supper* (1927), pp. 41-106.
Bard Thompson, pp. 141-56.

## a. *An Attack on the Canon of the Mass* (1523)

INTROIT
KYRIES
GLORIA IN EXCELSIS
COLLECT ⎫
EPISTLE ⎪
GRADUAL ⎬ BUT NONE FOR SAINTS' DAYS
GOSPEL ⎪
SERMON ⎭

NICENE CREED, DURING WHICH THERE IS
    PREPARATION OF THE ELEMENTS
SURSUM CORDA
PREFACE
SANCTUS

*The Canon is then replaced by the four following prayers:*

1 Most merciful and thrice holy Father, you created man in the beginning to enjoy paradise here and then afterwards to enjoy yourself. From this state of grace man fell through his own fault and was deemed worthy of death: he tainted all those who came after him; and then there was simply no hope of life, unless you, who alone are good, decided to relieve man's distress. You promised his seed that he would bruise the head of the evil seducer, so that man would not waste away in perpetual despair. In accordance with this promise, when the appointed time was fulfilled, you offered your Son, our Lord Jesus Christ, who took our flesh through the pure and ever-virgin Mary, that he might become for us perfect priest and perfect victim, unique among the human race. He gave himself to be the sacrifice for those who were lost: and not content with this, so that we might lack for nothing, he gave himself to be our food and drink. So, most blessed Father, we pray that your goodness may be constantly on our lips: and, although our deepest gratitude can never match your kindness, we pray that in your constant and unfailing goodness you will make us worthy to sing your praises continually with our hearts and lips and in our deeds, and to ask for nothing that would be alien to you. In confidence, therefore, we shall offer you prayer and praise in accordance with your will, as we have been taught by your most dearly beloved Son, Jesus Christ our Lord. Guided therefore by his precepts, we are bold to say:
    Our Father . . .

2 O God, you fed not only man from his youth but also every living creature. Feed our hungry souls, we pray, with heavenly food: for you are he who fills the hungry with good things. Our souls are spiritual, made in your image; therefore they can only be refreshed with spiritual food, and that food can only be given by your word. Your word is truth: for you are truth, and from you nothing can come

save that which is genuine, holy, steadfast and unspotted. Never deprive us of the food of your word, but ever feed us in your goodness. That is the true bread, which gives life to the world. We would eat the flesh and drink the blood of your Son in vain, if we did not firmly believe above all things through the faith of your word, that your Son our Lord Jesus Christ was crucified for us and atoned for the sins of the whole world. He himself said that the flesh profits nothing, but it is the Spirit which gives life. Quicken us, therefore, by your Spirit and never deprive us of your word; for your word is the vehicle of your Spirit, and assuredly it will never return to you empty. By that one thing, and that alone, is the human mind set free, for it is the truth; and you have promised through your Son that if the truth sets us free, then indeed we shall be truly free. So we pray that we may never lack the food of your word, for by that one thing we are granted the freedom and security of salvation. Through your Son, Jesus Christ our Lord, who is alive and reigns with you in the unity of the Holy Spirit, God, through all the ages of ages. Amen.

3   Therefore, O Lord, as you have taught us by your word that heaven and earth shall pass away rather than your word, so we firmly believe that not even the least particle will ever fall. And as we believe that your Son, once offered for us, made reconciliation to the Father, so we also firmly believe that he offered himself to be the food of our souls under the forms of bread and wine; so that the memory of his generous deed may never be abolished. Increase our faith, if it falters in any way; and grant that as your Son brought us back into your grace through the shame and bitterness of the cross and provided us with everlasting delights, so with him as leader and protector may we overcome the hardships and afflictions of this world, while we eat his body and drink his blood. For he gave himself to us as food, so that just as he himself vanquished the world, we, nourished by him, might hope to vanquish it in turn. In vain do we say that we make remembrance of him and what he did, if we do it by word alone. Grant us, therefore, merciful Father, through Christ your Son our Lord, through whom you give life to all things, and through whom you renew and sustain all things, that we may show him forth in our lives; so that the likeness which we lost in Adam may be restored. And in order that this may

take place in us the more effectively and surely, grant that all we who partake of the body and blood of your Son may have one hope and purpose, and be ourselves one in him, as he is one with you. Through the same Christ our Lord.

4  O God, among those born of women none has arisen greater than your Son, and you have deigned to reveal that he is the lamb to take away our sins. Through him be ready to hear our cry, 'O Lamb of God, you take away the sins of the world, have mercy on us.' In your kindness forgive all our faults. For he suffered, that through him we might have perpetual access to you: he wished to be clothed with our weakness, that in him we might have strength: he gave himself as food, that we might be nourished by him and grow into the fullness of his perfect life. O Lord, draw our hearts by your gracious light, that we may worthily and faithfully join in the sacred banquet of your Son, of which he himself is both our host and our most delectable food.

For on the night on which he was betrayed, he took bread, and giving thanks, he blessed and broke it, and gave it to his disciples, and said:

Take and eat. This is my body, which is given for you. Do this in remembrance of me.

Likewise the cup, after they had eaten; he took it, offered thanks, and gave it to them, saying:

Drink of this, all of you. For this is my blood of the new testament which is shed for you in the remission of sins. Do this, as often as you drink it, in remembrance of me.

For as often as you eat this bread and drink this cup, you proclaim the death of the Lord, until he comes.

Therefore come to me, all you who labour and are heavy laden, and I will give you rest.

The body of our Lord Jesus Christ preserve you to everlasting life.

The blood of our Lord Jesus Christ preserve you to everlasting life.

BRIEF THANKSGIVING
NUNC DIMITTIS
BLESSING

## b. *Action or Use of the Lord's Supper* (1525)

PREFACE
PRAYERS AND INTERCESSIONS
SERMON
CONFESSION OF SINS
PRAYER FOR PARDON
PREPARATION OF THE ELEMENTS
COLLECT
EPISTLE (I COR. 11.20-29)
GLORIA IN EXCELSIS (SAID ANTIPHONALLY)
GOSPEL (JOHN 6.47-63)
APOSTLES' CREED (SAID ANTIPHONALLY)
EXHORTATION (BY DEACON)
LORD'S PRAYER
PRAYER OF HUMBLE ACCESS (BY DEACON)

THE WAY CHRIST INSTITUTED THIS SUPPER
*The minister reads as follows:*

On the night when he was betrayed and given up to death, Jesus took bread; and when he had given thanks he broke it, and said, 'Take, eat; this is my body: do this in remembrance of me.' In the same manner also, he took the cup after supper, said thanks, and gave it to them, saying, 'Drink this, all of you: this cup is the new testament in my blood. Do this as often as you drink it, in remembrance of me. For as often as you eat this bread and drink this cup, you proclaim and glorify the Lord's death.'

*Then the designated servers carry around the unleavened bread, from which each one of the faithful takes a morsel or mouthful with his hand, or has it offered to him by the server who carries the bread around. And when those with the bread have proceeded so far that everyone has eaten his small piece, the other servers then follow with the cup, and in the same manner give it to each person to drink. And all of this takes place with such honour and propriety as well becomes the Church of God and the Supper of Christ.*

*Afterwards, the people having eaten and drunk, thanks is given according to the example of Christ, by the use of Psalm 112.*

POST-COMMUNION PSALM (SAID ANTIPHONALLY)
BRIEF THANKSGIVING
DISMISSAL

# 24

# Luther: a. *Formula Missae* 1523 and b. *Deutsche Messe* 1526

In 1520 Luther published his *Babylonish Captivity*, urging the need for a liturgy in the vernacular and attacking the Roman doctrines of transubstantiation and the sacrifice of the Mass. The liturgical expression of his views followed in 1523 in *Formula Missae*. This set out a truncated version of the Roman rite, and all that remained of the canon was the Sursum Corda, Institution Narrative, Sanctus and Benedictus accompanied by an elevation. After considerable experiment he produced his *Deutsche Messe* in 1526, in which the canon was reduced simply to the Institution Narrative. Both *Formulae Missae* and *Deutsche Messe* served as models for later Lutheran rites, and those which followed the latter were clearly slighter in content. The translation given here is from C. M. Jacobs *et al*, *The Works of Martin Luther*, 1932, vol. 6, pp. 83–117, 170–86.

BIBLIOGRAPHY

W. D. Maxwell, *An Outline of Christian Worship* (1945), pp. 73–80.

Luther D. Reed, *The Lutheran Liturgy* (1947), pp. 69–87.

Y. Brilioth, *Eucharistic Faith and Practice Evangelical and Catholic* (1930), pp. 94–144.

Bard Thompson, pp. 95–137.

Bouyer, pp. 384–91.

## a. *Formula of Mass and Communion for the Church at Wittenberg* 1523

. . . there follows that complete abomination, into the service of which all that precedes in the Mass has been forced, whence it is called *Offertorium*, and on account of which nearly everything sounds and reeks of oblation. In the midst of these things those words of life and salvation have been placed, just like in times past the ark of the Lord was placed in the temple of idols next to Dagon. And there is no Israelite there who is able either to approach or lead back the ark, until it has made its enemies infamous, smiting them on the back, with eternal shame, and has compelled them to send it away, which is a parable for the present time. Therefore repudiating all those things which smack of sacrifice and of the offertory, together with the entire *canon*, let us retain those things which are pure and holy, and then we will order our Mass in this fashion.

I   During the Creed or after the canon, let bread and wine be prepared in the customary way for consecration. Except that I am not yet fixed in my mind as to whether or not water should be mixed with the wine, although I incline to the preparation of pure wine, because the indication strikes me as wrong which Isaiah advances in Chapter 1, 'Your wine,' he says, 'is mixed with water.' For pure wine symbolizes beautifully the purity of the teaching of the Gospel. Then, too, nothing has been poured out for us save the blood of Christ only unmixed with ours, of which we make commemoration here. Neither can the dream of those stand who say that our union with Christ is here symbolized, the commemoration of which union we do not make here. Nor are we united before the shedding of his blood, otherwise at the same time we would be celebrating the pouring out of our own blood with the blood of Christ for ourselves. Nevertheless in opposition to liberty, I will not introduce a superstitious law. Christ will not care very much about this, nor are these matters worthy of contention. Enough foolish contention over this has been engaged in by the Roman and Greek churches as also in many other matters. And because some assert that blood and water flowed from the side of Christ, that does not prove anything. For that water signifies something other than what they wish to be signified by that mixed water. Nor was that mixed with the blood. Moreover the figure proves nothing, and the example does not stand; hence as a human invention it is held to be free.

II   The bread and the wine having been prepared, let the order be in this manner:

*The Lord be with you.*

Response: *And with thy spirit.*

*Lift up (your) hearts.*

Response: *Let us lift them up to the Lord.*
*Let us give thanks unto our Lord God.*
Response: *It is meet and right.*
*It is truly meet and right, just and salutary for us to give you thanks always*
*and everywhere, Holy Lord, Father Almighty, Eternal God, through*
*Christ our Lord.*

III   Then . . . *Who the day before he suffered took bread, giving thanks,*
*broke and gave to his disciples, saying, Take, eat. This is my body, which is*
*given for you.*
*Similarly also the cup, after he supped, saying, This cup is the new*
*testament in my blood which is poured out for you and for many in remission*
*of sins. As often as you shall do this, do it in memory of me.*

I wish these words of Christ, allowing a moderate pause after the
Preface, to be recited in the same tone of voice in which the Lord's
Prayer is sung at another place in the canon; so that it will be possible
for those standing by to hear, although in all these things liberty is
allowed to pious minds to recite these words either silently or audibly.

IV   The consecration ended, let the choir sing the Sanctus, and when
the Benedictus is sung, let the bread and chalice be elevated according
to the rite in use up to this time, chiefly on account of the infirm who
might be greatly offended by the sudden change in this more noted
rite in the Mass, especially where they have been taught through
vernacular sermons what is sought by this elevation.

V   After this the Lord's Prayer is read. Thus: *Let us pray: Taught by*
*your saving precepts,* etc., omitting the prayer following: *Deliver us, we*
*beseech,* with all signs, which they were wont to make over the host
and with the host over the chalice; nor shall the host be broken or
mixed in the chalice. But immediately after the Lord's Prayer shall be
said, *The Peace of the Lord,* etc., which is, so to speak, a public absolution
of the sins of the communicants, truly the Gospel voice announcing
remission of sins, the one and most worthy preparation for the Lord's
Table, if it be apprehended by faith and not otherwise than though it
came forth from the mouth of Christ himself. On account of this I
wish it to be announced with face turned to the people, as the bishops
were accustomed to do, which is the sole vestige of the ancient bishops
left among our bishops.

VI   Then let him communicate himself first, then the people; in the meanwhile let the Agnus Dei be sung. But if he should desire to pray the prayer, *O Lord Jesus Christ, Son of the living God, who according to the will of the Father,* etc. before communicating, he will not pray wrongly, only change the singular number to the plural *ours* and *us* for *mine* and *me.* Likewise the prayer, *The Body of the Lord,* etc. *guard* my *soul, or* your *soul unto life eternal. And the Blood of* our *Lord, guard* your *soul unto life eternal.*

VII   If he desires to sing the Communion let it be sung. But in the place of the *ad complendam* or final collect which so frequently savours of sacrifice, let this prayer be read in the same tone: *What we have taken with the mouth, O Lord.* This one also may be read: *Your Body, O Lord, which we have received,* etc. changing to the plural number. *Who live and reign,* etc. *The Lord be with you,* etc. In place of the *Ite missa,* let *Benedicamus domino* be said, adding Alleluia according to its own melodies where and when it is desired; or Benedicamus may be borrowed from Vespers.

VIII   Let the customary Benediction be given. Or take that from Numbers 6, which the Lord himself arranged and ordered: *The Lord bless us and guard us: May he show us his face and be merciful to us; The Lord turn his face to us and give us peace.* Or that in Psalm 96, *May God, our God, bless us: May God bless us and all the ends of the earth fear him. Amen.* I believe Christ used something of this kind when, ascending into heaven, he blessed his disciples.

And this, too, should be free to the bishop, namely, by what order he may desire either to receive or to administer both species. For assuredly he may consecrate both bread and wine consecutively before he receives the bread; or between the consecration of the bread and wine he may communicate with the bread both himself and as many as desire it, and thereupon consecrate the wine and at length give to all to drink of it. After which manner Christ seems to have acted, as the words of the Gospel reveal, where he commanded to eat the bread before he blessed the cup. Then is said expressly: *Likewise also the cup after he supped.* Thus you perceive the cup was blessed only after eating the bread. But this quite new rite will not permit the doing of those things following the consecration about which we spoke above, unless they should be changed.

This is the way we think about the Mass, but at the same time taking care in all such matters lest we make binding things which are free, or compel those to sin who either would do some other thing or omit certain things; only let them keep the words of consecration uncorrupted, and let them do this in faith. For these should be the usages of Christians, that is of children of the free woman, who observe these things voluntarily and from the heart, changing them as often as and in whatever manner they might wish. Wherefore it is not right that one should either require or establish some indispensable form as a law in this matter, by which he might ensnare or vex consciences. Whence also we find no complete example of this use in the ancient fathers and in the Primitive Church, save only in the Roman Church. But if they have appointed something as a law in this matter, it should not be observed; because these things neither can nor should be bound by laws . . .

## b. *The German Mass* 1526

GERMAN HYMN OR PSALM
KYRIES (THRICE)
SALUTATION AND COLLECT
EPISTLE
GERMAN HYMN
GOSPEL
APOSTLES' CREED AND THE PREPARATION OF THE ELEMENTS
SERMON
PARAPHRASE OF LORD'S PRAYER
EXHORTATION

*The Office and Consecration follows in this wise:*
*Example:* Our Lord Jesus Christ, in the night in which he was betrayed, took bread; and when he had given thanks, he brake it and gave it to his disciples, saying, Take, eat; this is my body, which is given for you; this do as oft as you do it, in remembrance of me.

After the same manner also, he took the cup, when he had supped, and said, Take and drink you all of it; this is the cup, a new testament in my blood, which is shed for you for the remission of sins; this do, as oft as you drink it, in remembrance of me.

It seems to me that it would be in accord with the institution of the Lord's Supper to administer the sacrament immediately after the consecration of the bread, before the cup is blessed, for both Luke and Paul say: He took the cup after they had supped, etc. During the distribution of the bread the German Sanctus could be sung, or the hymn, *Gott sei gelobet,* or the hymn of John Hus: *Jesus Christus unser Heiland.* Then shall the cup be blessed and administered; while the remainder of the hymns are sung, or the German Agnus Dei. Let there be a chaste and orderly approach, not men and women with each other but the women after the men, wherefore they should also stand separately at allotted places. What should be the attitude in respect to secret confession, I have indicated in other writings and my opinion can be found in the *Betbuechlein.*

We do not want to abolish the elevation but retain it because it goes well with the German Sanctus and signifies that Christ has commanded us to remember him. For as the sacrament is elevated in a material manner and yet Christ's body and blood are not seen in it, so he is remembered and elevated by the word of the sermon and is confessed and adored in the reception of the sacrament. Yet it is all apprehended by faith, for we cannot see how Christ gives his body and blood for us and even now daily shows and offers it before God to obtain grace for us.

### THE GERMAN SANCTUS

Isaiah, in a vision, saw the Lord
Enthroned, amid a heavenly light outpoured,
His garment's edge filled all the temple space.
The prophet's soul was filled with awe and grace.
Above the throne there stood two seraphim;
Each had six wings, his view disclosed to him.
With two they kept their faces veiled from view
And covered modestly their feet with two
While two served them in flight. To praise his name
They sang this hymn to God with loud acclaim:
Holy is God, the Lord of Sabaoth,
Holy is God, the Lord of Sabaoth,
Holy is God, the Lord of Sabaoth,
His glory hath gone forth o'er all the earth.
The clamour of their voices shook the place.
With haze and smoke the temple filled apace

### POST-COMMUNION COLLECT
### AARONIC BLESSING

# 25

# Olavus Petri: The Swedish Rite 1531

Liturgical reform in Sweden provides an interesting parallel with that in Germany. It was Lutheran in character and owed a great debt to Olavus Petri, who had been a student at Wittenberg from 1516 to 1518. His Swedish Mass appeared in 1531, five years after Luther's *Deutsche Messe*, and it was one of the most complete early Lutheran liturgies in the vernacular. Like Luther's it retained the traditional order of the medieval Mass, but removed everything relating to the Roman Offertory and Canon and placed the Sanctus after the Institution Narrative instead of after the Preface.

The work of Olavus Petri was continued by his younger brother Laurentius, Archbishop of Uppsala. He revised the 1531 rite five times before producing his own Church Order of 1571. While this remained distinctively Lutheran, it restored certain traditional features, principally the system of pericopes, the sermon, and the permissive use of Latin at such points as the Introit, the Gradual and the Creed.

BIBLIOGRAPHY

E. E. Yelverton, *The Mass in Sweden* (Henry Bradshaw Society, vol. 57, 1920).
Y. Brilioth, *Eucharistic Faith and Practice Evangelical and Catholic* (1930), pp. 231–253.
Luther D. Reed, *The Lutheran Liturgy* (1947), pp. 111–27.
Bouyer, pp. 396–407.

INVITATION AND CONFESSION
PRAYER OF FORGIVENESS AND GRACE
INTROIT
KYRIES
GLORIA IN EXCELSIS
SALUTATION
COLLECT
EPISTLE

GRADUAL HYMN
GOSPEL
APOSTLES' OR NICENE CREED

*Afterwards the priest commences the Preface, saying thus:*
    The Lord be with you.
    And with your spirit.
    Lift up your hearts to God.
    We lift up our hearts.
    Let us give thanks unto our Lord God.
    It is right and meet.

Truly it is meet, right and blessed that we should in all places give
you thanks and praise, holy Lord, almighty Father, everlasting God, for
all your benefits; and especially for that benefit which you gave us
when by reason of sins we were all in so bad a case that nothing but
damnation and eternal death awaited us, and no creature in heaven or
earth could help us. Then you sent forth your only-begotten son
Jesus Christ, who was of the same divine nature as yourself; you
suffered him to become a man for our sake; you laid our sins upon him;
and you suffered him to undergo death instead of our all dying eter-
nally. And as he has overcome death and risen again and now is alive
for evermore, so likewise shall all those who put their trust in him
overcome sin and death and through him attain to everlasting life. And
for our admonition that we should bear in mind and never forget his
benefit, in the night that he was betrayed, he celebrated a supper, in
which he took the bread in his holy hands, gave thanks to his heavenly
Father, blessed it, broke it, and gave it to his disciples, and said: Take
and eat; this is my body which is given for you; do this in remembrance of me.
*Then the priest lifts it up, lays it down again, and takes the cup, saying:*
    Likewise also he took the cup in his holy hands, gave thanks to his
heavenly Father, blessed it and gave it to his disciples and said: Take
and drink all of this; this is the cup of the new testament in my blood,
which is shed for you and for many for the remission of sins; as often
as you drink it, do this in remembrance of me.
*Then he lifts it up and sets it down again.*

*Afterwards is read or sung*

Holy, holy, holy, Lord God of Sabaoth; heaven and earth are full of your glory. Hosanna in the highest. Blessed is he who comes in the name of the Lord. Hosanna in the highest.

*Then the priest says:*

Let us all now pray as our Lord Jesus Christ himself has taught us, saying,

Our Father . . .

*Then the priest turns to the people and says:*

The peace of the Lord be with you.

And with your spirit.

AGNUS DEI

EXHORTATION (OPTIONAL)

*Afterwards he administers the bread to the people and says:*

The body of our Lord Jesus Christ preserve your soul unto ever-lasting life. Amen.

*Afterwards the cup, saying:*

The blood of our Lord Jesus Christ, etc.

HYMN OR NUNC DIMITTIS

SALUTATION

POST-COMMUNION COLLECT (FIXED)

BENEDICAMUS

AARONIC BLESSING

# 26

# Martin Bucer: The Strasbourg Rite 1539

The first revised rite in Strasbourg was the work of Diebold Schwarz, a former Dominican monk, and was first celebrated on 16 February 1524. It was an almost literal translation of the Roman rite, but excluding all references to the sacrifice of the Mass and the invocation of Mary and the saints. Shortly afterwards, however, Bucer began to make his influence felt, and after 1530 he become the accepted leader of the Reformers in the city. Thirteen revisions of the rite were made between 1526 and 1539, when he produced his service book *The Psalter, with complete Church Practice*. Its eucharistic rite exhibited his position as the via media between Luther and Zwingli, with a tendency towards greater simplicity and an increased emphasis on the didactic element. It had considerable influence on subsequent Calvinian (cf. pp. 139–42) and Scottish rites.

BIBLIOGRAPHY
W. D. Maxwell, *An Outline of Christian Worship* (1945), pp. 87–111.
　　*The Liturgical Portions of the Genevan Service Book* (1965), pp. 24–32, 188–98.
Bard Thompson, pp. 159–81.
G. J. Van de Poll, *Martin Bucer's Liturgical Ideas*, 1954.

## *The Psalter, with Complete Church Practice,*
## Strasbourg 1539

CONFESSION (3 FORMS)
ABSOLUTION OR WORD OF COMFORT
PSALM OR HYMN
KYRIE ELEISON (SOMETIMES)
GLORIA IN EXCELSIS (SOMETIMES)
PRAYER FOR ILLUMINATION
PSALM
GOSPEL

SERMON
EXHORTATION (OR BEFORE INSTITUTION NARRATIVE)
APOSTLES' CREED (OR PSALM OR HYMN)

PREPARATION OF THE ELEMENTS
*The Minister stands behind the Table and speaks to the people:*
    The Lord be with you
    Let us pray.
*Then he leads the prayer, with these or similar words:*
Almighty God, merciful God and Father, you have promised us
through your Son, that you will grant us whatever we ask of you in
his name; and you have also commanded us through your Spirit to
pray for those in authority and for all men. We heartily pray, through
your beloved Son our Saviour Jesus Christ, that you will enlighten
with the knowledge of your Gospel the hearts of our lord emperor and
king, all princes and nobles, and the magistrates and ruling body of this
city, that they and all those in power may acknowledge you as their
true and sovereign Lord, serve you with fear and trembling, and rule
over us, who are your handiwork and the sheep of your pasture,
according to your will and good pleasure.

Bring all men everywhere to the knowledge of the truth. In particular send upon this congregation, now assembled in your name, your
Holy Spirit, the Master and Teacher, that he may write your law upon
our hearts, take away our blindness, and lead us to acknowledge our
sin, which otherwise is death, and whose baseness and shame is hidden
from us. Make it clear to us, O Lord, and enlighten our eyes, that we
may see the truth and recognize that there is indeed nothing in us
except sin, death, hell and your deserved wrath. Grant that we may
hunger and thirst after the rich springs of your goodness and grace, and
gratefully receive of them what you have given to us through your
only-begotten Son, who, having become man like us poor sinners,
suffered, died and rose from the dead, that he might save us from sin,
death and hell, and bring us to the resurrection and our inheritance of
the kingdom of God.

Grant us, Lord and Father, that we may celebrate with true faith this
Supper of your dear Son, our Lord Jesus, as he has commanded, so that
we truly receive and enjoy the true communion of his body and blood,

of our Saviour himself, the truly heavenly bread of salvation. In this holy sacrament, he wills to offer and give himself so that he may live in us, and we in him, as members of his body, serving you fruitfully in every way for the building up of your Church, set free from every passion of our evil and corrupt flesh, from all anger, vexation, envy, hatred, selfishness, lewdness, unchastity, and any other wicked works of the flesh. So that we may, as your obedient children, always and in every way lift our hearts and souls to you with real childlike trust, and call upon you, saying as our Lord Jesus Christ, our only Master and Saviour, has taught us: Our Father . . .

*Another prayer*
Almighty, heavenly Father, you have promised through your Son, our Lord Jesus Christ, that you will give us whatever we ask in his name; and you have commanded us to pray for all men, and especially for those who are in authority. We therefore pray, dear and faithful Father, through your Son our Saviour, for our lord emperor and king, for all princes and nobles, and for all the magistrates of this city. Give your Spirit and a godly fear to those whom you have set to rule over us in your stead, that they may administer their office in accordance with your will and for your glory, that your children everywhere may lead calm and peaceful lives, in all godliness and propriety.

We also pray for all who are called to be pastors of your Church and proclaim your holy word. Grant them your word and Spirit that they may so serve you that all your elect may be drawn to you, and those who already bear your name and are counted as Christians may be true to their calling, promote your glory, and build up your Church.

We pray also for those whom you chasten through sickness and other adversity. Enable them to recognize your gracious hand and accept your discipline for their health's sake, that in your grace you may grant them comfort and help.

And we pray for those who have not yet heard your holy word, but remain in error and depravity. Enlighten their eyes that they recognize you as their God and creator, and accept your will.

We also pray, heavenly Father, for ourselves here present, that we may be gathered in your name. Drive from our hearts and souls all that displeases you. Help us to understand that in you we live and have our being; and that our sins are so heavy and grievous that only by the death of your Son, our Lord Jesus Christ, could we be restored to your life and grace. Help us to grasp by true faith how great is your love for us, that you have given your dear Son to die for us, so that when we believe in him we shall not perish but have everlasting life. Merciful God and Father, draw our hearts and souls to your Son, that as he gives himself to us in his holy Gospel and sacraments, and bestows his body and blood that we, corrupt as we are, may live in him, so may we receive a love such as his with lively faith and eternal gratitude, and so day by day increasingly die to all evil, grow and increase in all good-ness, and lead our lives in all soberness, patience and love towards our neighbour. It is to this that our Lord calls us and invites us through his holy Gospel and the sacraments. Wherefore, heavenly Father, grant that we may now receive and enjoy the same in true faith for our salvation, always as true and living members of him who is our Lord and your dear Son; and through him may we be your true and obedient children, always calling upon you and praying to you in a right Spirit and with truly faithful hearts: saying as he himself has taught us: Our Father . . .

## Another prayer

Almighty God and heavenly Father, you have promised through your dear Son, our Lord Jesus Christ, that you will grant to us whatever we ask in his Name. Your Son our Lord himself and his beloved apostles taught us to come together in his name, and promised to be there in the midst of us, and to obtain and procure for us from you whatever we on earth agree to ask of you. Especially he has commanded us to pray for those whom you have set over us as rulers and magistrates, and then for the needs both of your people and of all men. And since we have all gathered together as in your sight, to your praise, and in the name of your Son, our Lord Jesus: we heartily pray, merciful God and Father, through our only Saviour, your most beloved Son, that you will graciously forgive us all our sins and offences, and so lift our hearts and souls to you, that we may be able to ask and implore you with all our heart, according to your will and pleasure which alone are righteous.

Therefore, heavenly Father, we pray for our most gracious rulers, your servants, our lord emperor and king, and all princes, and nobles, and the magistrates of this city. Grant them always and increasingly the gift of your holy and right sovereign Spirit, that they may with a true faith acknowledge you as king of all kings, and lord of all lords, and your Son, our Lord Jesus, as him to whom you have given all power in heaven and on earth. May they so rule over their subjects, the work of your hands and the sheep of your pasture, in accordance with your good pleasure, that we both here and everywhere may lead a quiet, peaceful life in all godliness and sobriety, and by being delivered from the fear of our enemies, may serve you in all holiness and righteousness.

Furthermore, faithful Father and Saviour, we pray for all those you have appointed as pastors and curates of souls of your faithful people, and to whom you have entrusted the preaching of your holy Gospel. Give them increasingly your Holy Spirit, that they may be found faithful, always serving you in such a way that they may always gather your poor wandering sheep into the fold of Christ, your Son, their chief shepherd and bishop, and daily be built up by him into all holiness and righteousness, to the eternal praise of your name.

Merciful God and gracious Father, we also pray for all mankind. As it is your will to be known as a Saviour to the whole world, so draw to your Son, our Lord Jesus, those who are still estranged from him. And grant to those whom you have drawn to him and taught, that through him our only mediator, you will pardon sin and bestow every grace, that they may grow daily in such knowledge, and being filled with the fruit of all good works, may live without scandal, to your praise and the well-being of their neighbour, and await with confidence the advent and the day of your Son our Lord. And we pray especially for those whom you have disciplined, visiting and chastening them with poverty, misery, sickness, imprisonment and other adversities. Father of mercy and Lord of all consolation, may they recognize your gracious fatherly hand, that they may turn wholeheartedly to you, who alone chastens them, to receive from you as Father comfort and deliverance from all evil.

And may all of us, here gathered before you, in the name of your Son and at your table, O God and Father, truly and profoundly acknowledge the sin and depravity in which we were born, and into which we thrust ourselves more and more deeply by our sinful life. And since there is nothing good in our flesh, indeed since our flesh and blood cannot inherit your kingdom, grant that we may yield ourselves with all our hearts in true faith to your Son, our only Redeemer and Saviour. And since, for our sake, he has not only offered his body and blood upon the cross to you for our sin, but also wishes to give them to us for food and drink unto eternal life, grant that we may accept his goodness and gift with complete longing and devotion, and faithfully partake of and enjoy his true Body and true Blood – even himself, our Saviour, true God and true man, the only true bread from heaven; so that we may live no more in our sins and depravity, but that he may live in us and we in him – a holy, blessed and eternal life, verily partaking of the true and eternal testament, the covenant of grace, in sure confidence that you will be our gracious Father for ever, never again reckoning our sins against us, and in all things providing for us in body and soul, as your heirs and dear children: so that we may at all times give thanks and praise, and glorify your holy name in all that we say and do. Wherefore, heavenly Father, grant that we may celebrate today the glorious and blessed memorial of your dear Son our Lord and proclaim his death, so that we shall continually grow and increase in faith to you and in all goodness. So, in sure confidence, we call upon you now and always, God and Father, and pray as our Lord taught us to pray, saying: Our Father . . .

*At the conclusion of this prayer, the minister makes a short exhortation, if he has not done so at the end of the Sermon, to the effect that the Holy Supper is to be observed with true faith and meet devotion; and he explains this Mystery.*

*After such an exhortation and explanation, the minister reads the words of the Lord, as the holy Evangelists and Paul have recorded them.*

## THE INSTITUTION OF THE LORD'S SUPPER

In the same night in which the Lord Jesus was betrayed, while they were eating, he took the bread, and brake it, and gave it to his disciples, and said: Take, eat, this is my body which is given for you; do this in remembrance of me. In the same manner he also took the cup after the supper, gave thanks, and offered it to them, and said: Drink this all of you; this is the new testament in my blood, which is shed for you and for many for the forgiveness of sins; do this, as often as you drink it, in remembrance of me.

*Forthwith the minister speaks in these words:*

Believe in the Lord, and give eternal praise and thanks unto him!

*Herewith he distributes the bread and cup of the Lord, first saying these words:*

Remember, believe and proclaim that Christ the Lord has died for you.

*Thereupon the church sings 'Gott sey gelobet' or another psalm appropriate to the occasion.*

PRAYER OF THANKSGIVING (3 FORMS)
AARONIC BLESSING
DISMISSAL

# 27

# John Calvin: *Form of Church Prayers,* Geneva 1542

John Calvin's rite first appeared when he was minister to the congregation of French exiles at Strasbourg from 1538 to 1541. Impressed by Bucer's German rite which he found in use there, he adopted it almost word for word in French. His Geneva rite was first published in 1542 after his recall. It was a slightly simplified form of his Strasbourg rite; but the matter was essentially the same. In structure it also resembled Farel's rite, which it replaced at Geneva.

The rite was intended to recover the eucharist in its primitive simplicity as the weekly worship of the Church. Such a service, Calvin believed, would 'manifest God's glory and allow the sweetness of consolation to fill the hearts of the faithful better than all the childish and theatrical follies of the mass' (Brilioth p. 172). The canon was replaced by the Narrative of the Institution, followed by a reminder of God's promises, an excommunication of those forbidden to communicate and a prayer for worthy reception.

BIBLIOGRPAHY
Bard Thompson, pp. 185–210.
Y. Brilioth, *Eucharistic Faith and Practice Evangelical and Catholic* (1930), pp. 164–79.
W. D. Maxwell, *An Outline of Christian Worship* (1945), pp. 112–19.
   *The Liturgical Portions of the Genevan Service Book* (1965), pp. 17–36.
A. Barclay, *The Protestant Doctrine of the Lord's Supper* (1927).

SCRIPTURE SENTENCE – PSALM 124.8
CONFESSION
PRAYER FOR PARDON
METRICAL PSALM
PRAYER FOR ILLUMINATION
LESSON
SERMON

INTERCESSIONS
PARAPHRASE OF THE LORD'S PRAYER
APOSTLES' CREED
PLACING OF BREAD AND WINE ON THE TABLE

*After the Prayer and the Confession of Faith, to testify in the name of the people that all wish to live and die in the doctrine of Christ, he (the minister) says aloud:*

Let us listen to the institution of the Holy Supper by Jesus Christ, as narrated by St Paul in the eleventh chapter of the first epistle to the Corinthians:

For I have received from the Lord what I also delivered to you, that the Lord Jesus, on the night when he was betrayed, took bread, and when he had given thanks, he broke it, and said, 'This is my body, which is broken for you. Do this in remembrance of me.' In the same way also the cup, after supper, saying, 'This cup is the new covenant in my blood. Do this, as oft as you drink it, in remembrance of me.' For as often as you eat this bread and drink the cup, you proclaim the Lord's death until he comes. Whoever, therefore, eats the bread or drinks the cup of the Lord in an unworthy manner will be guilty of profaning the body and blood of the Lord. Let a man examine himself, and so eat of the bread and drink of the cup. For anyone who eats and drinks without discerning the body eats and drinks judgement upon himself.

We have heard, brethren, how our Lord celebrated his Supper with his disciples, and thereby indicating that strangers, namely those who are not of the company of the faithful, ought not to be admitted. Therefore, in accordance with this rule, in the name and by the authority of the Lord Jesus Christ, I excommunicate all idolaters, blasphemers, despisers of God, heretics, and all who form private sects to break the unity of the Church, all perjurers, all who rebel against parents or their superiors, all who are seditious, mutinous, quarrelsome or brutal, all adulterers, fornicators, thieves, misers, ravishers, drunkards, gluttons, and all who lead a scandalous life. I declare that they must abstain from this holy table, for fear of defiling and contaminating the holy food which our Lord Jesus Christ gives only to his household and believers.

Therefore, in accordance with the exhortation of St Paul, let each man prove and examine his conscience, to see whether he has truly repented of his faults, and is satisfied with himself, desiring to live henceforth a holy life and according to God. Above all, let each man see whether he puts his trust in the mercy of God, and seeks his salvation entirely in Jesus Christ; and whether, renouncing all hatred and rancour, he truly intends and resolves to live in peace and brotherly love with his neighbours.

If we have this testimony in our hearts before God, let us have no doubt at all that he claims us for his children, and that the Lord Jesus Christ addresses his words to us, to invite us to his table, and to present us with this holy sacrament which he communicated to his disciples.

And although we may feel within ourselves much frailty and misery from not having perfect faith, and from being inclined to unbelief and distrust, as well as from not being devoted to the service of God so entirely and with such zeal as we ought, and from having to war daily against the lusts of our flesh, nevertheless, since our Lord has graciously permitted us to have his gospel imprinted on our hearts, in order to withstand all unbelief, and has given us the desire and longing to renounce our own desires, in order to follow righteousness and his holy commandments, let us all be assured that the sins and imperfections which remain in us will not prevent him from receiving us, and making us worthy to partake of this spiritual table: for we do not come to declare that we are perfect or righteous in ourselves; but, on the contrary, by seeking our life in Christ, we confess that we are in death. Let us therefore understand that this sacrament is a medicine for the spiritually poor and sick, and that the only worthiness which our Saviour requires in us is to know ourselves, so as to be dissatisfied with our vices, and have all our pleasure, joy and contentment in him alone.

First, then, let us believe in those promises which Jesus Christ, who is the unfailing truth, has pronounced with his own lips, namely, that he is indeed willing to make us partakers of his own body and blood, in order that we may possess him entirely and in such a manner that he may live in us, and we in him. And although we see only bread and wine, yet let us not doubt that he accomplishes spiritually in our souls all that he shows us outwardly by these visible signs; in other words, that he is heavenly bread, to feed and nourish us unto eternal life.

Next, let us not be unmindful of the infinite goodness of our Saviour, who displays all his riches and blessings at this table, in order to give them to us; for, in giving himself to us, he bears testimony to us that all which he has is ours. Moreover, let us receive this sacrament as a pledge that the virtue of his death and passion is imputed to us for righteousness, just as if we had suffered it in our own persons. Let us never be so perverse as to hold back when Jesus Christ invites us so gently by his word. But, reflecting on the dignity of the precious gift which he gives us, let us present ourselves to him with ardent zeal, in order that he may make us capable of receiving him.

With this in mind, let us raise our hearts and minds on high, where Jesus Christ is, in the glory of his Father, and from whence we look for him at our redemption. Let us not be bemused by these earthly and corruptible elements which we see with the eye, and touch with the hand, in order to seek him there, as if he were enclosed in the bread or wine. Our souls will only then be disposed to be nourished and vivified by his substance, when they are raised above all earthly things, and carried as high as heaven, to enter the kingdom of God where he dwells. Let us therefore be content to have the bread and the wine as signs and evidences, spiritually seeking the reality where the word of God promises that we shall find it.

*This done, the ministers distribute the bread and cup to the people, having warned them to come forward with reverence and in order. Meanwhile some psalms are sung, or some passage of scripture read, suitable to what is signified by the sacrament.*

EXHORTATION
PRAYER OF THANKSGIVING
HYMN OF PRAISE
AARONIC BLESSING

# 28

# Hermann: *A Simple and Religious Consultation* 1545

Hermann von Wied, Archbishop-Elector of Cologne, was noted for the efficient manner in which he administered his archdiocese: discipline was improved and liturgical reforms were introduced. Initially hostile to the Reformers, he gradually mellowed; and in 1542 he invited Bucer and Melancthon to assist in schemes for further reform. His reforming zeal eventually met with hostility from the Emperor Charles V and Pope Paul III, who excommunicated and deposed him in 1546.

His proposals for reform appeared in 1543 under the title *Einfältiges Bedenken*. This was revised and translated into Latin in 1545 as *Simplex ac Pia Deliberatio*, and an English translation first appeared in 1547 as *A Simple and Religious Consultation*. Although it was never used in Cologne, Cranmer borrowed extensively from it in *The Order of the Communion 1548*.

The translation is that published anonymously in 1548, with the spelling modernized and the variant readings of the first edition (1547) added in the notes.

BIBLIOGRAPHY

H. A. Wilson, *The Order of the Communion (1548)* (Henry Bradshaw Society, vol. 34, 1908).

Cuming, pp. 44–5.

F. E. Brightman, *The English Rite* (1915), 2 vols.

## Of the Preparation to the Supper of the Lord
### (to be used the night before the celebration)

PSALM

ANTIPHON AND HYMN

MAGNIFICAT

COLLECT

PSALM

NEW TESTAMENT LESSON

SERMON

EXHORTATION

PRAYERS

PRIVATE CONFESSION


## How the Lord's Supper must be Celebrated

CONFESSION

COMFORTABLE WORDS

ABSOLUTION

INTROIT

KYRIES

GLORIA IN EXCELSIS

COLLECT

EPISTLE

ALLELUIA (OR GRAIL OR SEQUENCE)

GOSPEL

SERMON

PRAYER 'FOR ALL STATES OF MEN AND NECESSITIES OF THE CON-
GREGATION'

ALTERNATIVE SHORTER FORM OF PRAYER

CREED

OFFERTORY

WARNING AGAINST UNWORTHY RECEPTION AND NON-COM-
MUNICATING ATTENDANCE

*But howsoever the rest be handled in the congregation at this time, they
nevertheless that shall be admitted to the communion, as soon as they have*

*made their oblation, must go together to that place that shall be appointed unto them, nigh to the altar. For in every temple there must some place be appointed nigh the altar for them which shall communicate at the Lord's table, according to the opportunity and fitness of every temple. They, then, which shall be admitted to the communion of the Lord's board shall stand in that place, the men in their proper place and the women in their place, and there they shall give thanks and pray religiously with the pastor. The giving of thanks shall be handled after the accustomed manner, but in Douch,[1] that the people universally may give thanks to the Lord, as both the example and the commandment of the Lord requireth, and also the old Church observed.*

*The priest:* The Lord be with you.

*The people:* And with thy spirit.

*The priest:* Lift up your hearts.

*The people:* We have unto the Lord.

*The priest:* Let us give thanks unto the Lord our God.

*The people:* It is meet and right.

*The priest:*

It is verily a thing worthy, right, meet, and wholesome, that we give thanks unto thee always and everywhere, that we praise and magnify thee, Lord, holy Father, Almighty, everlasting God, through Jesus Christ our Lord, by whom thou madest us of nothing unto thine image, and hast appointed all other creatures to our uses; and whereas we, through the sin of Adam sliding from thee, were made thine enemies, and therefore subject to death and eternal damnation, thou of thy infinite mercy and unspeakable love, didst send the same thy Son, the eternal Word, into this world; who through the cross and death delivered us from sins and the power of the devil, and brought us again into thy favour by his holy Spirit whom he sent unto us from thee; and gave his body and blood to be the food of a new and eternal life, that, being more confirmed through the trust of thy mercy and love, we should ever go forward to all that that is thy pleasure by renewing and sanctifying of ourselves; and that we should glorify and exalt thee here and evermore in all our words and deeds, and sing unto thee without end with all thy holy angels and beloved children.

*After these things,* Sanctus *shall be sung; where clerks be, in Latin, but of the people in Douch,[1] one side answering the other, thrice of both parts. As*

1. i.e. in German.

*for that that is wont to be added, 'The Lord God of hosts' and Benedictus, it shall be sung communally of the whole congregation, and therefore in Douch.*

*Straightway after this, let the priest sing the words of the Lord's Supper in Douch, 'Our Lord, the night in which he was delivered,' etc. But these words must be sung of the priest with great reverence and plainly, that they may be well understanded of all men. And the people shall say to these words, Amen, which all the old churches observed, and the Greeks do yet observe the same. For the whole substance of this sacrament is contained in these words. And it consisteth altogether in the true understanding and faith of these words that the sacrament be wholesomely administered and received.*

*After[2] the people then have answered their Amen, the priest shall add:*
Let us pray.
Our Father, which art in heaven, etc.
*To which prayer of the Lord the people shall say again their Amen.*
*The priest:*    The Lord's peace be ever with you.
*The people:*    And with thy spirit.
*After this, they which be admitted to the communion and do look for the same in their place shall come to the Lord's board religiously in order, first men and then women; and the whole sacrament shall be given to them all, that they may be partakers of the body and blood of the Lord, receiving not only bread but also the cup, even as he instituted it.*

*At the exhibition of the body let the pastor say:*
Take and eat to thy health the body of the Lord, which was delivered for thee.[3]

*At the exhibition of the cup:*
Take and drink to thy health the blood of the Lord, which was shed for thy sins.

*After the communion, let Agnus Dei be sung both in Douch and Latin, one side answering the other, where clerks be. And then let this Douch song be sung, 'Gott sei gelobet,' item, 'Jesus Christus unser Heiland,' if the communion of the sacraments shall give so much time and leisure.*

*When the communion is ended, let the priest sing, turning to the people:*
The Lord be with you.

2. Latin: *Postquam;* 1547 and 1548: *when.*
3. Latin: *pro te;* 1547 and 1548: *for thy sins.*

*The people:* And with thy spirit.

*The priest:* Let us pray.

Almighty, everlasting God, we give thanks to thy exceeding goodness, because thou hast fed us with the body of thy only-begotten Son our Lord and given us his blood to drink. We humbly beseech thee, work in us with thy Spirit, that, as we have received this divine sacrament with our mouths, so we may also receive and ever hold fast with true faith thy grace, remission of sins, and communion with Christ thy Son. All which things thou hast exhibited unto us in these sacraments through our Lord Jesus Christ thy Son, which liveth and reigneth with thee in unity of the holy Ghost, very God and very man, for ever. Amen.

*Another thanksgiving:*

We give thee thanks, Father, Almighty God, which hast refreshed us with the singular gift of thy body and blood; we beseech thy goodness that the same may help to confirm our faith in thee, and to kindle mutual love among us, by the same our Lord Jesus Christ, etc.

*Last of all, let the pastor bless the people with these words:*

The Lord bless thee and keep thee; the Lord lighten his countenance upon thee and have mercy on thee; the Lord lift up his face upon thee and settle thee in peace. Amen.

*Or thus.*

God have mercy upon us and bless us, lighten his countenance upon us, and give us his peace. Amen.

*Or thus.*

God, the Father, the Son, and the holy Ghost, bless and keep us. Amen.

*Or thus.*

The blessing of God, the Father, the Son, and the Holy Ghost, be with us and remain with us for ever. Amen.

FINAL RUBRICS

# 29

## The Order of the Communion 1548

One of the first steps in liturgical reform in the reign of Edward VI was the work produced by a commission of bishops and scholars and printed in March 1548 under the title *The Order of the Communion*. It provided for the communion of the laity in both kinds and encouraged a proper preparation for communion. The order was to be used in the Roman rite immediately after the priest's own communion. It was closely modelled on Hermann von Wied's *A Simple and Religious Consultation* (cf. pp. 143–7). *The Order of the Communion* was eventually incorporated into the rite of the 1549 Prayer Book.

BIBLIOGRAPHY
H. A. Wilson, *The Order of the Communion (1548)*, (Henry Bradshaw Society, vol. 34, 1908).
Cuming, pp. 61–5.
F. E. Brightman, *The English Rite* (1915), 2 vols.

EXHORTATION TO PREPARE FOR COMMUNION
*The time of the Communion shall be immediately after that the priest himself hath received the sacrament, without the varying of any other rite or ceremony in the Mass, until other order shall be provided; but as heretofore usually the priest hath done with the sacrament of the Body, to prepare, bless, and consecrate so much as will serve the people, so it shall continue still after the same manner and form, save that he shall bless and consecrate the biggest chalice, or some fair and convenient cup or cups, full of wine with some water put into it; and that day not drink it up all himself, but, taking only one sup or draught, leave the rest upon the altar covered, and turn to them that are disposed to be partakers of the Communion, and shall thus exhort them as followeth.*
    Dearly beloved in the Lord . . . all the days of our life.
*Then shall the priest say to them which be ready to take the sacrament:*

If any man here be an open blasphemer, adulterer, in malice, or envy, or any other notable crime, and be not truly sorry therefore, and earnestly minded to leave the same vices, or that doth not trust himself to be reconciled to almighty God, and in charity with all the world, let him yet a while bewail his sins and not come to this holy table, lest after the taking of this most blessed bread, the devil enter into him, as he did into Judas, to fulfill in him all iniquity, and to bring him to destruction, both of body and soul.

*Here the priest shall pause a while to see if any man will withdraw himself: and if he perceive any so to do, then let him commune with him privily at convenient leisure, and see whether he can with good exhortation bring him to grace: and after a little pause, the priest shall say:*

You that do truly and earnestly repent you of your sins and offences, committed to almighty God, and be in love and charity with your neighbours, and intend to lead a new life and heartily to follow the commandments of God, and to walk from henceforth in his holy ways, draw near, and take this holy Sacrament to your comfort, make your humble confession to almighty God, and to his holy Church, here gathered together in his name, meekly kneeling upon your knees.

*Then shall a general confession be made in the name of all those that are minded to receive the holy Communion, either by one of them, or else by one of the ministers, or by the priest himself, all kneeling humbly upon their knees.*

Almighty God, father of our Lord Jesus Christ, maker of all things, judge of all men, we acknowledge and bewail our manifold sins and wickedness, which we from time to time most grievously have committed by thought, word and deed against thy divine majesty, provoking most justly thy wrath and indignation against us: we do earnestly repent, and be heartily sorry for these our misdoings; the remembrance of them is grievous unto us; the burden of them is intolerable; have mercy upon us, have mercy upon us, most merciful father, for thy son our Lord Jesus Christ's sake. Forgive us all that is past, and grant that we may ever hereafter, serve and please thee in newness of life, to the honour and glory of thy name, through Jesus Christ our Lord.

*Then shall the priest stand up, and turning him to the people, say thus:*

Our blessed Lord, who hath left power to his Church to absolve penitent sinners from their sins, and to restore to the grace of the heavenly father such as truly believe in Christ, have mercy upon you, pardon and deliver you from all sins, confirm and strengthen you in all goodness, and bring you to everlasting life.

*Then shall the priest stand up and turning him toward the people, say thus:*

Hear what comfortable words our Saviour Christ saith to all that truly turn to him.

Come unto me all that travail and be heavy laden and I shall refresh you. God so loved the world that he gave his only begotten son, to the end that all that believe in him should not perish, but have life everlasting.

Hear also what S. Paul saith.

This is a true saying, and worthy of all men to be embraced and received, that Jesus Christ came into this world to save sinners.

Hear also what S. John saith.

If any man sin, we have an advocate with the Father, Jesus Christ the righteous, he it is that obtained grace for our sins.

*Then shall the priest kneel down and say in the name of all them that shall receive the Communion this prayer following.*

We do not presume to come to this thy table (O merciful Lord) trusting in our own righteousness, but in thy manifold and great mercies; we be not worthy so much as to gather up the crumbs under the table. But thou art the same Lord, whose property is always to have mercy: Grant us therefore gracious Lord so to eat the flesh of thy dear son Jesus Christ, and to drink his blood in these holy mysteries, that we may continually dwell in him, and he in us, that our sinful bodies may be made clean by his body, and our souls washed through his most precious blood. Amen.

*Then shall the priest rise, the people still reverently kneeling; and the priest shall deliver the Communion, first to the ministers, if any be there present, that they may be ready to help the priest, and after to the others. And when he doth deliver the Sacrament of the body of Christ, he shall say to every one these words following.*

The body of our Lord Jesus Christ, which was given for thee, preserve thy body unto everlasting life.

*And the priest delivering the Sacrament of the blood, and giving every one to drink once and no more, shall say:*

The blood of our Lord Jesus Christ, which was shed for thee, preserve thy soul unto everlasting life.

*If there be a deacon or other priest, then shall he follow with the chalice, and as the priest ministereth the bread, so shall he for more expedition minister the wine, in form before written.*

*Then shall the priest, turning him to the people, let the people depart with this blessing:*

The peace of God which passeth all understanding, keep your hearts and minds in the knowledge and love of God, and of his son Jesus Christ, our Lord.

*To the which the people shall answer* Amen.

*Note, that the bread that shall be consecrated shall be such as heretofore hath been accustomed. And every of the said consecrated breads shall be broken in two pieces at the least, or more, by the discretion of the minister, and so distributed. And men must not think less to be received in part than in the whole, but in each of them the whole body of our Saviour Jesus Christ.*

*Note, that if it doth so chance, that the wine hallowed and consecrated doth not suffice or be enough for them that do take the Communion, the priest after the first cup or chalice be emptied, may go again to the altar, and reverently and devoutly prepare and consecrate another, and so the third, or more likewise, beginning at these words,*

Simili modo, postquam cenatum est, *and ending at these words* qui pro uobis et pro multis effundetur in remissionem peccatorum, *and without any elevation or lifting up.*

# 30

## The Book of Common Prayer 1549

The preparation of the first Book of Common Prayer was undertaken by Archbishop Cranmer and 'certain of the most learned and discreet bishops and other learned men of this realm', known as the Windsor Commission. It was meant to be a congregational book, written in the vernacular and grounded in scripture. The eucharist kept the structure of the Roman rite, preserved prayers of traditional English usage and included the Order of the Communion of 1548. It required communion in both kinds, and made no provision for private Masses. The Act of Uniformity of January 1549 ordered that it should come into use on the Feast of Pentecost (9 June), or if copies were available earlier, three weeks after the copy had been procured. The earliest existing copies, printed by Edward Whitchurche, were dated 7 March.

BIBLIOGRAPHY

*The First and Second Prayer Books of King Edward the Sixth* (Everyman edition edited by D. E. W. Harrison, 1972).

E. C. Ratcliff, *The Booke of Common Prayer: its Making and Revisions 1549–1661* (Alcuin Club Collections No. 37, 1949).

F. E. Brightman, *The English Rite* (1915), 2 vols.

Cuming, pp. 32–96.

C. H. Smyth, *Cranmer and the Reformation under Edward VI* (1972).

Jasper Ridley, *Thomas Cranmer* (1962), pp. 272–89.

Horton Davies, *Worship and Theology in England. Vol. 1 From Cranmer to Hooker 1534–1603* (1970), pp. 3–39, 76–123, 165–201.

Bouyer, pp. 407–17.

## The Supper of the Lord, and the Holy Communion, commonly called the Mass

INTRODUCTORY RUBRICS
INTROIT PSALM (CLERKS)

LORD'S PRAYER (PRIEST)

COLLECT FOR PURITY (PRIEST)

INTROIT PSALM (PRIEST)

KYRIES (NINEFOLD)

GLORIA IN EXCELSIS

SALUTATION AND COLLECT OF THE DAY

COLLECT FOR THE KING

EPISTLE

GOSPEL

NICENE CREED

SERMON OR HOMILY

EXHORTATIONS (OPTIONAL)

OFFERTORY WITH SENTENCES

*While the Clerks do sing the offertory, so many as are disposed shall offer to the poor men's box, every one according to his ability and charitable mind. And at the offering days appointed, every man and woman shall pay to the Curate the due and accustomed offerings.*

*Then so many as shall be partakers of the holy communion shall tarry still in the quire, or in some convenient place nigh the quire, the men on the one side, and the women on the other side. All other (that mind not to receive the said holy communion) shall depart out of the quire, except the Ministers and Clerks.*

*Then shall the Minister take so much bread and wine as shall suffice for the persons appointed to receive the holy communion, laying the bread upon the corporas, or else in the paten, or in some other comely thing prepared for that purpose: and putting the wine into the chalice, or else in some fair or convenient cup prepared for that use (if the chalice will not serve) putting thereto a little pure and clean water, and setting both the bread and wine upon the altar. Then the Priest shall say,*

|   |   |
|---|---|
|  | The Lord be with you. |
| *Answer:* | And with thy spirit. |
| *Priest:* | Lift up your hearts. |
| *Answer:* | We lift them up unto the Lord. |
| *Priest:* | Let us give thanks to our Lord God. |
| *Answer:* | It is meet and right so to do. |
| *The Priest:* | It is very meet, right, and our bounden duty that we |

should at all times and in all places give thanks to thee, O Lord, holy Father, almighty everlasting God.

*Here shall follow the proper Preface, according to the time (if there be any specially appointed), or else immediately shall follow,*

Therefore with angels, etc.

## Proper Prefaces

*Upon Christmas Day*

Because thou didst give Jesus Christ thine only Son to be born as this day for us; who, by the operation of the Holy Ghost, was made very man of the substance of the Virgin Mary his mother; and that without spot of sin, to make us clean from all sin. Therefore, etc.

*Upon Easter Day*

But chiefly are we bound to praise thee for the glorious resurrection of thy Son Jesus Christ our Lord: for he is the very paschal Lamb, which was offered for us, and hath taken away the sin of the world; who by his death hath destroyed death, and by his rising to life again hath restored to us everlasting life. Therefore, etc.

*Upon the Ascension Day*

Through thy most dear beloved Son Jesus Christ our Lord; who, after his most glorious resurrection, manifestly appeared to all his disciples, and in their sight ascended up into heaven to prepare a place for us; that where he is, thither might we also ascend, and reign with him in glory. Therefore, etc.

*Upon Whit Sunday*

Through Jesus Christ our Lord; according to whose most true promise the Holy Ghost came down this day from heaven with a sudden great sound, as it had been a mighty wind, in the likeness of fiery tongues, lighting upon the apostles, to teach them, and to lead them to all truth, giving them both the gift of divers languages, and also boldness with fervent zeal constantly to preach the gospel unto all nations; whereby we are brought out of darkness and error into the clear light and true knowledge of thee, and of thy Son Jesus Christ. Therefore, etc.

*Upon the feast of the Trinity*

It is very meet, right, and our bounden duty, that we should at all times and in all places, give thanks to thee, O Lord, Almighty, everlasting God, which art one God, one Lord; not one only Person, but three Persons in one substance. For that which we believe of the glory of the Father, the same we believe of the Son, and of the Holy Ghost, without any difference or inequality. Whom with angels, etc.

*After which Preface shall follow immediately,*

Therefore with angels and archangels, and with all the holy company of heaven, we laud and magnify thy glorious name; evermore praising thee, and saying,

Holy, holy, holy, Lord God of hosts: heaven and earth are full of thy glory. Hosannah in the highest. Blessed is he that cometh in the name of the Lord. Glory to thee, O Lord, in the highest.

*This the Clerks shall also sing.*

*When the Clerks have done singing, then shall the Priest or Deacon turn him to the people, and say,*

Let us pray for the whole state of Christ's Church.

*Then the priest, turning him to the altar, shall say or sing, plainly and distinctly, this prayer following,*

Almighty and everliving God, which by thy holy apostle hast taught us to make prayers, and supplications, and to give thanks for all men; We humbly beseech thee most mercifully to receive these our prayers, which we offer unto thy divine Majesty; beseeching thee to inspire continually the universal church with the spirit of truth, unity, and concord: and grant, that all they that do confess thy holy name may agree in the truth of thy holy word, and live in unity and godly love. Specially we beseech thee to save and defend thy servant Edward our king; that under him we may be godly and quietly governed; and grant unto his whole council, and to all that be put in authority under him, that they may truly and indifferently minister justice, to the punishment of wickedness and vice, and to the maintenance of God's true religion and virtue. Give grace (O heavenly Father) to all bishops, pastors and curates that they may both by their life and doctrine set forth thy true and lively word, and rightly and duly administer thy holy sacraments. And to all thy people give thy heavenly grace; that with meek heart and due reverence, they may hear and receive thy holy word; truly serving thee in holiness and righteousness all the days of their life. And we most humbly beseech thee of thy goodness (O Lord) to comfort and succour all them, which in this transitory life be in trouble, sorrow, need, sickness, or any other adversity. And especially we commend unto thy merciful goodness this congregation, which is here assembled in thy name, to celebrate the commemoration of the most glorious death of thy Son. And here we do give unto thee most high praise, and hearty thanks, for the wonderful grace and virtue declared in thy saints, from the beginning of the world; and chiefly in the glorious and most blessed Virgin Mary, mother of thy Son Jesu Christ our Lord and God; and in the holy patriarchs, prophets, apostles and martyrs, whose examples (O Lord) and stedfastness in thy faith, and keeping thy holy commandments, grant us to follow. We commend unto thy mercy (O Lord) all other thy servants, which are departed hence from us with the sign of faith, and now do rest in the sleep of peace: grant unto them, we beseech thee, thy mercy, and everlasting peace; and that, at the day of the general resurrection, we and all they which be of the mystical body of thy Son, may altogether be set on his right hand, and hear that his most joyful voice, Come unto me, O ye that be blessed of my Father, and possess the kingdom, which is prepared for you from the beginning of the world. Grant this, O Father, for Jesus Christ's sake, our only Mediator and Advocate.

O God, heavenly Father, which of thy tender mercy didst give thine only Son Jesu Christ to suffer death upon the cross for our redemption; who made there (by his one oblation once offered) a full, perfect, and sufficient sacrifice, oblation, and satisfaction, for the sins of the whole world; and did institute, and in his holy gospel command us to celebrate a perpetual memory of that his precious death, until his coming again: hear us (O merciful Father) we beseech thee; and with thy Holy Spirit and word vouchsafe to ble✠ss and sanc✠tify these thy gifts and creatures of bread and wine, that they may be unto us the body and blood of thy most dearly beloved Son Jesus Christ, who, in the same night that he was betrayed, took bread;[1] and when he had

1. Here the priest must take the bread into his hands.

blessed, and given thanks, he brake it, and gave it to his disciples, saying, Take, eat; this is my body which is given for you; do this in remembrance of me.

Likewise after supper he took the cup,[2] and when he had given thanks, he gave it to them, saying, Drink ye all of this; for this is my blood of the new Testament, which is shed for you and for many for remission of sins. Do this, as oft as you shall drink it, in remembrance of me.

*These words before rehearsed are to be said, turning still to the altar, without any elevation or shewing the sacrament to the people.*

Wherefore, O Lord and heavenly Father, according to the institution of thy dearly beloved Son our Saviour Jesu Christ, we thy humble servants do celebrate and make here before thy divine Majesty, with these thy holy gifts, the memorial which thy Son hath willed us to make; having in remembrance his blessed passion, mighty resurrection, and glorious ascension; rendering unto thee most hearty thanks for the innumerable benefits procured unto us by the same; entirely desiring thy fatherly goodness mercifully to accept this our sacrifice of praise and thanksgiving; most humbly beseeching thee to grant, that by the merits and death of thy Son Jesus Christ and through faith in his blood, we and all thy whole church may obtain remission of our sins, and all other benefits of his passion. And here we offer and present unto thee (O Lord) our self, our souls and bodies, to be a reasonable, holy and lively sacrifice unto thee; humbly beseeching thee, that whosoever shall be partakers of this holy communion may worthily receive the most precious body and blood of thy Son, Jesus Christ, and be fulfilled with thy grace and heavenly benediction, and made one body with thy Son Jesu Christ, that he may dwell in them, and they in him. And although we be unworthy (through our manifold sins) to offer unto thee any sacrifice, yet we beseech thee to accept this our bounden duty and service, and command these our prayers and supplications, by the ministry of thy holy angels, to be brought up into thy holy tabernacle, before the sight of thy divine Majesty; not weighing our merits, but pardoning our offences, through Christ our Lord; by whom, and with whom, in the unity of the Holy Ghost, all honour

2. Here the priest shall take the cup into his hands.

and glory be unto thee, O Father Almighty, world without end.
Amen.

Let us pray.

As our Saviour Christ hath commanded and taught us, we are bold
to say, Our Father, which art in heaven, hallowed be thy name. Thy
kingdom come. Thy will be done in earth, as it is in heaven. Give us
this day our daily bread. And forgive us our trespasses, as we forgive
them that trespass against us. And lead us not into temptation.

*The Answer.*   But deliver us from evil.

*Then shall the Priest say,*
            The peace of the Lord be alway with you.
*The Clerks:* And with thy spirit.
*The Priest:*   Christ our Paschal Lamb is offered up for us, once for all,
when he bare our sins on his body upon the cross; for he is the very
Lamb of God that taketh away the sins of the world: therefore let us
keep a joyful and holy feast with the Lord.

*Here the Priest shall turn him toward those that come to the holy communion,
and shall say,*

You that do truly and earnestly repent you of your sins to Almighty
God, and be in love and charity with your neighbours, and intend to
lead a new life, following the commandments of God, and walking
from henceforth in his holy ways; Draw near, and take this holy
sacrament to your comfort; make your humble confession to Almighty
God, and to his holy church here gathered together in his name,
meekly kneeling upon your knees.

*Then shall this general confession be made, in the name of all those that are
minded to receive the holy communion, either by one of them, or else by one
of the Ministers, or by the Priest himself, all kneeling humbly upon their
knees.*

Almighty God, Father of our Lord Jesus Christ, Maker of all things,
Judge of all men; we acknowledge and bewail our manifold sins and
wickedness, which we, from time to time, most grievously have committed, by thought, word, and deed, against thy divine Majesty, provoking most justly thy wrath and indignation against us. We do

earnestly repent, and be heartily sorry for these our misdoings; the remembrance of them is grievous unto us; the burden of them is intolerable. Have mercy upon us, have mercy upon us, most merciful Father; for thy Son our Lord Jesus Christ's sake, forgive us all that is past; and grant that we may ever hereafter serve and please thee in newness of life, to the honour and glory of thy name; through Jesus Christ our Lord.

*Then shall the Priest stand up, and turning himself to the people, say thus:*

Almighty God, our heavenly Father, who of his great mercy hath promised forgiveness of sins to all them which with hearty repentance and true faith turn unto him; Have mercy upon you; pardon and deliver you from all your sins; confirm and strengthen you in all goodness; and bring you to everlasting life; through Jesus Christ our Lord. Amen.

*Then shall the Priest say.*

Hear what comfortable words our Saviour Christ saith to all that truly turn to him.

Come unto me all that travail, and be heavy laden, and I shall refresh you. So God loved the world, that he gave his only-begotten Son, to the end that all that believe in him should not perish, but have life everlasting.

Hear also what Saint Paul saith.

This is a true saying, and worthy of all men to be received, that Jesus Christ came into this world to save sinners.

Hear also what Saint John saith.

If any man sin, we have an Advocate with the Father, Jesus Christ the righteous; and he is the propitiation for our sins.

*Then shall the Priest, turning him to God's board, kneel down, and say in the name of all that receive the communion, this prayer following:*

We do not presume to come to this thy table (O merciful Lord) trusting in our own righteousness, but in thy manifold and great mercies. We be not worthy so much as to gather up the crumbs under thy table; but thou art the same Lord whose property is always to have mercy: Grant us therefore (gracious Lord) so to eat the flesh of thy dear Son Jesus Christ, and to drink his blood, in these holy mysteries, that we may continually dwell in him, and he in us, that our sinful bodies may be made clean by his body, and our souls washed through his most precious blood. Amen.

*Then shall the Priest first receive the communion in both kinds himself, and next deliver it to other Ministers, if any be there present (that they may be ready to help the chief Minister), and after to the people. And when he delivereth the sacrament of the body of Christ, he shall say to every one these words:*

The body of our Lord Jesus Christ, which was given for thee, preserve thy body and soul unto everlasting life.

*And the Minister delivering the sacrament of the blood, and giving every one to drink once, and no more, shall say,*

The blood of our Lord Jesus Christ, which was shed for thee, preserve thy body and soul unto everlasting life.

*If there be a Deacon or other Priest, then shall he follow with the chalice; and as the Priest ministereth the sacrament of the body, so shall he (for more expedition) minister the sacrament of the blood, in form before written.*

*In the communion time the Clerks shall sing,*

ii   O Lamb of God, that takest away the sins of the world; Have mercy upon us.

O Lamb of God, that takest away the sins of the world; Grant us thy peace.

*Beginning so soon as the Priest doth receive the holy communion, and when the communion is ended, then shall the Clerks sing the post-communion.*

POST-COMMUNION SENTENCES
PRAYER OF THANKSGIVING
BLESSING
FINAL RUBRICS AND COLLECTS

# 31

# *The Book of Common Prayer* 1552

The 1549 Prayer Book was not well received: traditionalists objected to the changes in the Mass; while the Reformers, such as Hooper and Ridley, did not regard the changes as far-reaching enough. A thorough-going criticism of the Book was submitted by Martin Bucer in his *Censura* in 1551: and in the spring of 1552 a second Prayer Book, much more Protestant in tone, appeared. Under a new Act of Uniformity its use was required by All Saints Day. It had a short life, however; for on the death of Edward VI in July 1553 and the accession of Mary, the Roman rite was restored as the official use.

BIBLIOGRAPHY

*The First and Second Prayer Books of King Edward the Sixth* (Everyman edition edited by D. E. W. Harrison, 1972).

E. C. Ratcliff, *The Booke of Common Prayer: its Making and Revisions 1549–1661* (Alcuin Club Collections No. 37, 1949).

F. E. Brightman, *The English Rite*, (1915), 2 vols.

Cuming, pp. 96–116.

C. H. Smyth, *Cranmer and the Reformation under Edward VI* (1972).

Jasper Ridley, *Thomas Cranmer* (1962), pp. 290–342.

Horton Davies, *Worship and Theology in England. Vol. 1 From Cranmer to Hooker 1534–1603* (1970), pp. 3–39, 76–123, 194–210.

C. W. Dugmore, 'The First Ten Years, 1549–1559' in *The English Prayer Book 1549–1662*, essays published for the Alcuin Club (1963), pp. 6–30.

E. C. Whitaker, *Martin Bucer and the Book of Common Prayer* (Alcuin Club Collections No. 55, 1974).

# The Order for the Administration of the Lord's Supper of Holy Communion

INTRODUCTORY RUBRICS
LORD'S PRAYER (PRIEST)

COLLECT FOR PURITY (PRIEST)
TEN COMMANDMENTS
COLLECT OF THE DAY
COLLECT FOR THE KING
EPISTLE
GOSPEL
NICENE CREED
SERMON OR HOMILY
NOTICES
OFFERTORY WITH SENTENCES
PRAYER FOR THE CHURCH MILITANT
EXHORTATIONS
INVITATION    'YE THAT DO TRULY . . .'
CONFESSION    'ALMIGHTY GOD, FATHER OF OUR LORD . . .'
ABSOLUTION    'ALMIGHTY GOD, OUR HEAVENLY FATHER...'
COMFORTABLE WORDS

*After which the Priest shall proceed, saying,*
          Lift up your hearts.
*Answer:*   We lift them up unto the Lord.
*Priest:*   Let us give thanks unto our Lord God.
*Answer:*   It is meet and right so to do.
*Priest:*   It is very meet, right, and our bounden duty, that we should at all times, and in all places, give thanks unto thee, O Lord, holy Father, almighty, everlasting God.

*Here shall follow the proper Preface, according to the time (if there be any especially appointed), or else immediately shall follow,*
     Therefore with angels, etc.

PROPER PREFACES
*Upon Christmas Day, and seven days after*
  'Because thou didst give Jesus Christ . . .'
*Upon Easter Day, and seven days after*
  'But chiefly are we bound to praise thee . . .'
*Upon the Ascension Day, and seven days after*
  'Through thy most dearly beloved Son, Jesus Christ . . .'

*Upon Whit Sunday, and six days after*
'Through Jesus Christ our Lord, according . . .'
*Upon the feast of Trinity only*
'Who art one God, one Lord . . .' (omitting 'holy Father')

*After which Preface shall follow immediately*
Therefore with angels and archangels, and with all the company of heaven, we laud and magnify thy glorious name, evermore praising thee, and saying,

Holy, holy, holy, Lord God of hosts, heaven and earth are full of thy glory. Glory be to thee, O Lord most high.

*Then shall the Priest, kneeling down at God's board, say, in the name of all them that shall receive the communion, this prayer following:*
We do not presume to come to this thy table (O merciful Lord) trusting in our own righteousness, but in thy manifold and great mercies. We be not worthy so much as to gather up the crumbs under thy table; but thou art the same Lord whose property is always to have mercy: Grant us therefore (gracious Lord) so to eat the flesh of thy dear Son Jesus Christ, and to drink his blood, that our sinful bodies may be made clean by his body, and our souls washed through his most precious blood, and that we may evermore dwell in him, and he in us. Amen.

*Then the Priest, standing up, shall say as followeth:*
Almighty God, our heavenly Father, which of thy tender mercy didst give thine only Son Jesus Christ to suffer death upon the cross for our redemption; who made there (by his one oblation of himself once offered) a full, perfect, and sufficient sacrifice, oblation, and satisfaction for the sins of the whole world; and did institute, and in his holy gospel command us to continue, a perpetual memory of that his precious death until his coming again; Hear us, O merciful Father, we beseech thee; and grant that we, receiving these thy creatures of bread and wine, according to thy Son our Saviour Jesus Christ's holy institution, in remembrance of his death and passion, may be partakers of his most blessed body and blood; who, in the same night that he was betrayed, took bread; and when he had given thanks, he brake it, and gave it to his disciples, saying, Take, eat; this is my body which is given for you. Do this in remembrance of me. Likewise after

supper he took the cup; and when he had given thanks, he gave it to them, saying, Drink ye all of this; for this is my blood of the New Testament, which is shed for you and for many for remission of sins: do this, as oft as ye shall drink it in remembrance of me.

*Then shall the Minister first receive the communion in both kinds himself, and next deliver it to other Ministers, if any be there present (that they may help the chief Minister), and after to the people in their hands kneeling. And when he delivereth the bread he shall say,*

Take and eat this, in remembrance that Christ died for thee, and feed on him in thy heart by faith with thanksgiving.

*And the Minister that delivereth the cup, shall say,*

Drink this in remembrance that Christ's blood was shed for thee, and be thankful.

*Then shall the Priest say the Lord's Prayer, the people repeating after him every petition.*

*After shall be said as followeth:*

O Lord and heavenly Father, we thy humble servants entirely desire thy fatherly goodness mercifully to accept this our sacrifice of praise and thanksgiving; most humbly beseeching thee to grant, that by the merits and death of thy Son Jesus Christ, and through faith in his blood, we and all thy whole church may obtain remission of our sins, and all other benefits of his passion. And here we offer and present unto thee, O Lord, ourselves, our souls and bodies, to be a reasonable, holy, and lively sacrifice unto thee; humbly beseeching thee, that all we which be partakers of this holy communion, may be fulfilled with thy grace and heavenly benediction. And although we be unworthy, through our manifold sins to offer unto thee any sacrifice, yet we beseech thee to accept this our bounden duty and service; not weighing our merits, but pardoning our offences, through Jesus Christ our Lord; by whom, and with whom in the unity of the Holy Ghost, all honour and glory be unto thee, O Father Almighty, world without end. Amen.

*or* PRAYER OF THANKSGIVING
GLORIA IN EXCELSIS
BLESSING
FINAL RUBRICS AND COLLECTS

# 32

# John Knox: *The Form of Prayers and Ministration of the Sacraments* 1556

In 1555 John Knox was banished from Frankfurt-on-Main and went to Geneva, where he became minister to a congregation of English exiles. Here *The Form of Prayers and Ministration of the Sacraments,* the first Reformed rite in English, was published in the following year. Clearly it owed a great deal to Calvin's rite of 1542, and the influence of the 1552 Prayer Book was also evident in the exhortation before Communion. Nevertheless it showed a degree of independence in providing new intercessions and a new consecration prayer, although both were Calvinistic in tone and content. The book came into general use in Scotland after Knox's return there in 1559.

BIBLIOGRAPHY

W. D. Maxwell, *The Liturgical Portions of the Genevan Service Book* (1965).
    *An Outline of Christian Worship* (1945), pp. 120–5.
G. B. Burnet, *The Holy Communion in the Reformed Church of Scotland* (1960), pp. 1–25.
J. M. Barkley, *The Worship of the Reformed Church* (1966), pp. 22–6.
Bard Thompson, pp. 287–307.

CONFESSION OF SIN (2 FORMS)

PSALM

PRAYER FOR ILLUMINATION

LESSON

SERMON

INTERCESSIONS

LORD'S PRAYER

APOSTLES' CREED

PSALM DURING WHICH THE ELEMENTS ARE BROUGHT FORWARD

*The Minister:* Institution Narrative from 1 Cor. 11
　　　　　　Exhortation

*The exhortation ended, the minister cometh down from the pulpit, and sitteth at the Table, every man and woman in like wise taking their places as occasion best serveth, then he taketh bread and giveth thanks, either in these words following, or like in effect:*

O Father of mercy and God of all consolation, seeing all creatures do acknowledge and confess thee, as governor, and lord, it becometh us the workmanship of thine own hands, at all times to reverence and magnify thy godly majesty, first that thou hast created us to thine own Image and similitude: but chiefly that thou hast delivered us, from that everlasting death and damnation into the which Satan drew mankind by the means of sin: from the bondage whereof (neither man nor angel was able to make us free) but thou (O Lord) rich in mercy and infinite in goodness, hast provided our redemption to stand in thy only and well-beloved son: whom of very love thou didst give to be made man, like unto us in all things (sin except) that in his body he might receive the punishments of our transgression, by his death to make satisfaction to thy justice, and by his resurrection to destroy him that was author of death, and so to reduce and bring again life to the world, from which the whole offspring of Adam most justly was exiled.

O Lord we acknowledge that no creature is able to comprehend the length and breadth, the deepness and height, of that thy most excellent love which moved thee to show mercy, where none was deserved; to promise and give life, where death had gotten victory: but to receive us into thy grace, when we would do nothing but rebel against thy justice.

O Lord the blind dullness of our corrupt nature will not suffer us sufficiently to weigh these thy most ample benefits: yet nevertheless at the commandment of Jesus Christ our Lord, we present ourselves to this his table (which he hath left to be used in remembrance of his death until his coming again) to declare and witness before the world, that by him alone we have received liberty, and life: that by him alone, thou dost acknowledge us thy children and heirs: that by him alone, we have entrance to the throne of thy grace: that by him alone, we are possessed in our spiritual kingdom, to eat and drink at his table: with whom we have our conversation presently in heaven, and by whom our bodies shall be raised up again from the dust, and shall be placed with him in that endless joy, which thou (O father of mercy) prepared for thine elect, before the foundation of the world was laid.

And these most inestimable benefits, we acknowledge and confess to have received of thy free mercy and grace, by thy only beloved son Jesus Christ, for the which therefore we thy congregation moved by thy holy spirit render thee all thanks, praise, and glory for ever and ever.

*This done, the Minister breaketh the bread and delivereth it to the people, who distribute and divide the same amongst themselves, according to our saviour Christ's commandment, and in like wise giveth the cup. During the which time, some place of the scriptures is read, which doth lively set forth the death of Christ, to the intent that our eyes and senses may not only be occupied in these outward signs of bread and wine, which are called the visible word: but that our hearts and minds also may be fully fixed in the contemplation of the Lord's death which is by this holy Sacrament represented. And after the action is done, he giveth thanks, saying . . .*

PRAYER OF THANKSGIVING
PSALM 103
BLESSING

# 33

# The Scottish Prayer Book of 1637

Both Charles I and Archbishop Laud desired to unite the Churches of England and Scotland; and as one step in this direction they encouraged the introduction of a new service book to replace *The Book of Common Order*. Two Scottish bishops, Maxwell of Ross and Wedderburn of Dunblane, were primarily responsible for the work, although Laud and Wren probably contributed in the final stages. The book was approved by Charles in April 1636, but its introduction in Scotland in the spring of 1637 was bitterly opposed. In 1638 the General Assembly repudiated the Book, abolished episcopacy and ratified the National Covenant. The 1637 Liturgy was an attempt to restore many of the features of 1549, although at the same time it contained many distinctive Scottish features. It was in many ways a fine piece of work and undoubtedly influenced both the revisers of 1662 and the compilers of the later Scottish rite of 1764.

BIBLIOGRAPHY

G. Donaldson, *The Making of the Scottish Prayer Book of 1637* (1954).

W. J. Grisbrooke, *Anglican Liturgies of the Seventeenth and Eighteenth Centuries* (Alcuin Club Collections No. 40, 1958), pp. 1–18, 163–82.

G. W. Sprott (editor), *Scottish Liturgies of the Reign of James VI* (1901).

## The Scottish Prayer Book of 1637

INTRODUCTORY RUBRIC

LORD'S PRAYER (PRESBYTER)

COLLECT FOR PURITY

TEN COMMANDMENTS

COLLECT FOR THE KING

COLLECT OF THE DAY

EPISTLE

GOSPEL

NICENE CREED

SERMON (OR HOMILY OR EXHORTATION)

OFFERTORY WITH SENTENCES

PRAYER FOR THE CHURCH MILITANT

EXHORTATIONS (2)

*Then shall the Presbyter say to them that come to receive the holy Communion, this invitation.*

    You that do truly and earnestly . . .

*Then shall this general Confession be made, in the name of all those that are minded to receive the holy Communion, by the Presbyter himself, or the Deacon; both he and all the people kneeling humbly upon their knees.*

    Almighty God, Father of our Lord Jesus Christ, maker of all things, judge of all men . . .

*Then shall the Presbyter, or the Bishop (being present), stand up, and, turning himself to the people, pronounce the Absolution, as followeth.*

    Almighty God our heavenly Father, who of his great mercy . . .

*Then shall the Presbyter also say*

    Hear what comfortable words our Saviour Christ saith unto all that truly turn to him . . .

*After which the Presbyter shall proceed, saying:*

        Lift up your hearts.

*Answer:*    We lift them up unto the Lord.

*Presbyter:* Let us give thanks unto our Lord God.

*Answer:*    It is meet and right so to do.

*Presbyter:* It is very meet, right, and our bounden duty, that we should at all times, and in all places, give thanks unto thee, O Lord, holy Father, Almighty, everlasting God.

*Here shall follow the proper Preface, according to the time, if there be any especially appointed; or else immediately shall follow,*

    Therefore with Angels and Archangels, etc.

**PROPER PREFACES**

*Upon Christmas Day, and seven days after*

Because thou didst give Jesus Christ . . .

*Upon Easter Day, and seven days after*

But chiefly are we bound to praise thee . . .

*Upon Ascension Day, and seven days after*

Through thy most dearly-beloved Son Jesus Christ our Lord . . .

*Upon Whitsunday, and six days after*

Through Jesus Christ our Lord: according to whose most true promise . . .

*Upon the Feast of Trinity only*

It is very meet, and our bounden duty . . .

*After which Prefaces shall follow immediately this Doxology*

Therefore with Angels and Archangels, and with all the company of heaven, we laud and magnify thy glorious Name, evermore praising thee, and saying, Holy, holy, holy, Lord God of hosts. Heaven and earth are full of thy glory. Glory be to thee, O Lord most high.

*Then the Presbyter, standing up, shall say the Prayer of Consecration, as followeth. But then, during the time of Consecration, he shall stand at such a part of the holy Table, where he may with more ease and decency use both his hands.*

Almighty God, our heavenly Father, which of thy tender mercy didst give thy only Son Jesus Christ to suffer death upon the cross for our redemption; who made there (by his one oblation of himself once offered) a full, perfect, and sufficient sacrifice, oblation, and satisfaction for the sins of the whole world, and did institute, and in his holy gospel command us to continue, a perpetual memory of that his precious death and sacrifice, until his coming again: Hear us, O merciful Father, we most humbly beseech thee, and of thy Almighty goodness vouchsafe so to bless and sanctify with thy word and Holy Spirit these thy gifts and creatures of bread and wine, that they may be unto us the body and blood of thy most dearly beloved Son; so that we, receiving them according to thy Son our Saviour Jesus Christ's holy institution, in remembrance of his death and passion, may be partakers of the same his most precious body and blood: Who, in the night that he was betrayed, *took bread*,[1] and when he had given thanks, he brake it, and gave it to his disciples, saying, Take, eat, this is my body, which is given for you: do this in remembrance of me. Likewise after supper he *took the cup*,[2] and when he had given thanks, he gave it to them, saying, Drink ye all of this, for this is my blood of the new testament which is shed for you, and for many, for the remission of sins: do this, as oft as ye shall drink it, in remembrance of me.

*Immediately after shall be said this Memorial or Prayer of Oblation, as followeth*

Wherefore, O Lord and heavenly Father, according to the institution of thy dearly-beloved Son, our Saviour Jesus Christ, we thy humble servants do celebrate and make here before thy Divine Majesty with these thy holy gifts, the memorial which thy Son hath willed us to make; having in remembrance his blessed passion, mighty resurrection, and glorious ascension; rendering unto thee most hearty thanks for the innumerable benefits procured unto us by the same. And we entirely desire thy Fatherly goodness mercifully to accept this our sacrifice of praise and thanksgiving, most humbly beseeching thee to grant, that by the merits and death of thy Son Jesus Christ, and through faith in his blood, we and all thy whole Church may obtain remission of our sins, and all other benefits of his passion. And here we offer and present unto thee, O Lord, ourselves, our souls and bodies, to be a reasonable, holy, and lively sacrifice unto thee; humbly beseeching thee, that whosoever shall be partakers of this holy Communion, may worthily receive the most precious body and blood of thy Son Jesus Christ, and be fulfilled with thy grace and heavenly benedictions, and made one body with him, that he may dwell in them, and they in him. And although we be unworthy, through our manifold sins, to offer unto thee any sacrifice: yet we beseech thee to accept this our bounden duty and service, not weighing our merits, but pardoning our offences, through Jesus Christ our Lord: by whom, and with whom, in the unity of the Holy Ghost, all honour and glory be unto thee, O Father Almighty, world without end. Amen.

1. *At these words* took bread *the Presbyter that officiates is to take the paten in his hand.*
2. *At these words* took the cup *he is to take the chalice in his hand, and lay his hand upon so much, be it in chalice or flagons, as he intends to consecrate.*

*Then shall the Presbyter say*

As our Saviour Christ hath commanded and taught us, we are bold to say,

Our Father, which art in heaven . . . Amen.

*Then shall the Presbyter, kneeling down at God's board, say in the name of all them that shall communicate, this Collect of humble access to the holy Communion, as followeth.*

We do not presume to come to this thy table (O merciful Lord) trusting in our own righteousness . . . evermore dwell in him, and he in us. Amen.

*Then shall the Bishop, if he be present, or else the Presbyter that celebrateth first receive the Communion in both kinds himself, and next deliver it to the other Bishops, Presbyters and Deacons (if any be there present), that they may help him that celebrateth; and after to the people in due order, all humbly kneeling. And when he receiveth himself, or delivereth the bread to others, he shall say this benediction:*

The body of our Lord Jesus Christ, which was given for thee, preserve thy body and soul unto everlasting life.

*Here the party receiving shall say, Amen.*

*And the Presbyter or Minister that receiveth the cup himself, or delivereth it to others, shall say this benediction.*

The blood of our Lord Jesus Christ, which was shed for thee, preserve thy body and soul unto everlasting life.

*Here the party receiving shall say, Amen.*


COLLECT OF THANKSGIVING

GLORIA IN EXCELSIS

BLESSING

ABLUTIONS AND FINAL RUBRICS

COLLECTS

# 34

## The Westminster Directory 1644

After the overthrow of King Charles I, Parliament set up at Westminster a commission composed mainly of Presbyterians with a minority of Independents and assisted by Scottish representatives to produce a form of church government, a confession of faith, and forms of worship. In 1644 it produced a *Directory for the Public Worship of God*, which was received by Parliament on 3 January, 1645. At the same time the use of the Book of Common Prayer was abolished. The *Directory* attempted to comprehend the virtues of form and freedom, but it met with a mixed reception. Inevitably it was disliked intensely by Anglicans, while Independents regarded it as too precise.

BIBLIOGRAPHY

T. Leishman, *The Westminster Directory* (1901). (This text, which is used here, is in modern spelling.)

Bard Thompson, pp. 354–71. (The text with the original spelling.)

Horton Davies, *The Worship of the English Puritans* (1948).

G. B. Burnet, *The Holy Communion in the Reformed Church of Scotland* (1900), pp. 105–11.

E. C. Ratcliff, 'Puritan Alternatives to the Prayer Book: The *Directory* and Richard Baxter's *Reformed Liturgy*', in *The English Prayer Book 1549–1662*, essays published for the Alcuin Club (1963), pp. 56–74.

OF THE ASSEMBLING OF THE CONGREGATION, AND THEIR BE-
HAVIOUR IN THE PUBLIC WORSHIP OF GOD
*The Congregation being assembled, the Minister, after solemnly calling on
them to the worshipping of the great name of God, is to begin with Prayer . . .*

OF THE PUBLIC READING OF THE HOLY SCRIPTURES
*All the Canonical Books of the Old and New Testament (but none of those
which are commonly called Apocrypha) shall be publicly read in the vulgar
tongue, out of the best allowed translation, distinctly, that all may hear and
understand.*

OF PUBLIC PRAYER BEFORE THE SERMON
*After Reading of the Word (and Singing of the Psalm), the Minister who is to
preach, is to endeavour to get his own and his hearers' hearts to be rightly
affected with their sins, that they may all mourn in sense thereof before the
Lord, and hunger and thirst after the grace of God in Jesus Christ, by proceeding to a more full Confession of sin, with shame and holy confusion of face,
and to call upon the Lord to this effect: –*

(The text includes not only confession but also intercession and prayer
for grace.)

*We judge this to be a convenient order, in the ordinary Public Prayers; yet
so, as the Minister may defer (as in prudence he shall think meet) some part
of these Petitions till after his Sermon, or offer up to God some of the Thanksgivings hereafter appointed in his Prayer before his Sermon.*

OF THE PREACHING OF THE WORD
*Ordinarily, the subject of his Sermon is to be some text of Scripture, holding
forth some principle or head of religion, or suitable to some special occasion
emergent; or he may so go on in some Chapter, Psalm, or Book of the Holy
Scripture, as he shall see fit . . .*

OF PRAYER AFTER THE SERMON
The prayers after the Sermon are to include Thanksgivings and
petitions, with special reference to the subject of the Sermon. *And
because the Prayer which Christ taught His Disciples is not only a pattern*

*of prayer, but itself a most comprehensive prayer, we recommend it also to be used in the Prayers of the Church.*

*And whereas, at the Administration of the Sacraments, the holding public Fasts and days of Thanksgiving, and other special occasions, which may afford matter of special petitions and thanksgivings, it is requisite to express somewhat in our Public Prayers (as at this time it is our duty to pray for a blessing upon the Assembly of Divines, the armies by sea and land, for the defence of the King, Parliament, and Kingdom), every Minister is herein to apply himself in his Prayer, before or after his Sermon, to those occasions: but, for the manner, he is left to his liberty, as God shall direct and enable him in piety and wisdom to discharge his duty.*

*The Prayer ended, let a Psalm be sung, if with convenience it may be done. After which (unless some other Ordinance of Christ, that concerneth the Congregation at that time, be to follow) let the Minister dismiss the Congregation with a solemn Blessing.*

OF THE CELEBRATION OF THE COMMUNION, OR SACRAMENT OF THE LORD'S SUPPER

*The Communion, or Supper of the Lord, is frequently to be celebrated; but how often, may be considered and determined by the Ministers, and other Church-governors of each congregation, as they shall find most convenient for the comfort and edification of the people committed to their charge. And, when it shall be administered, we judge it convenient to be done after the Morning Sermon.*

*The ignorant and the scandalous are not fit to receive this Sacrament of the Lord's Supper.*

*Where this Sacrament cannot with convenience be frequently administered, it is requisite that public warning be given the Sabbath day before the administration thereof; and that either then, or on some day of that week, something concerning that Ordinance, and the due preparation thereunto, and participation thereof, be taught; that, by the diligent use of all means sanctified of God to that end, both in public and private, all may come better prepared to that heavenly Feast.*

*When the day is come for administration, the Minister, having ended his Sermon and Prayer, shall make a short Exhortation,*

'Expressing the inestimable benefit we have by this Sacrament, together with the ends and use thereof: setting forth the great necessity of having our comforts and strength renewed thereby in this our pilgrimage and warfare: how necessary it is that we come unto it with knowledge, faith, repentance, love and with hungering and thirsting souls after Christ and His benefits; how great the danger to eat and drink unworthily.

'Next, he is, in the name of Christ, on the one part, to warn all such as are ignorant, scandalous, profane, or that live in any sin or offence against their knowledge or conscience, that they presume not to come to that holy Table; showing them, that he that eateth and drinketh unworthily, eateth and drinketh judgment unto himself: And, on the other part, he is in especial manner to invite and encourage all that labour under the sense of the burden of their sins, and fear of wrath, and desire to reach out unto a greater progress in grace than yet they can attain unto, to come to the Lord's Table; assuring them in the same name, of ease, refreshing, and strength to their weak and wearied souls.'

*After this exhortation, warning, and invitation, the Table being before decently covered, and so conveniently placed, that the Communicants may orderly sit about it, or at it, the Minister is to begin the action with sanctifying and blessing the elements of Bread and Wine set before him (the Bread in comely and convenient vessels, so prepared that, being broken by him, and given, it may be distributed among the Communicants; the Wine also in large cups), having first, in a few words, showed, that those elements, otherwise common, are now set apart and sanctified to his holy use, by the Word of Institution and Prayer.*

*Let the Words of Institution be read out of the Evangelists, or out of the first Epistle of the Apostle Paul to the Corinthians, chap. xi. 23. I have received of the Lord, etc., to the 27th verse, which the Minister may, when he seeth requisite, explain and apply.*

*Let the Prayer, Thanksgiving, or Blessing of the Bread and Wine, be to this effect:*

'With humble and hearty acknowledgment of the greatness of our misery, from which neither man nor angel was able to deliver us, and of our great unworthiness of the least of all God's mercies: To give thanks to God for all His benefits, and especially for that great benefit of our redemption, the love of God the Father, the sufferings and merits of the Lord Jesus Christ the Son of God, by which we are delivered; and for all means of grace, the Word and Sacraments; and for this Sacrament in particular, by which Christ, and all His benefits, are applied and sealed up unto us, which, notwithstanding the denial of them unto others, are in great mercy continued unto us, after so much and long abuse of them all.

'To profess that there is no other name under heaven by which we can be saved, but the Name of Jesus Christ, by whom alone we receive liberty and life, have access to the throne of grace, are admitted to eat and drink at His own Table, and are sealed up by His Spirit to an assurance of happiness and everlasting life.

'Earnestly to pray to God, the Father of all mercies, and God of all consolation, to vouchsafe His gracious presence, and the effectual working of His Spirit in us; and so to sanctify these elements both of Bread and Wine, and to bless His own Ordinance, that we may receive by faith the Body and Blood of Jesus Christ, crucified for us, and so to feed upon Him, that He may be one with us, and we with Him; that He may live in us, and we in Him, and to Him who hath loved us, and given Himself for us.'

*All which he is to endeavour to perform with suitable affections, answerable to such an holy Action, and to stir up the like in the people.*

*The elements being now sanctified by the Word and Prayer, the Minister, being at the Table, is to take the Bread in his hand and say, in these expressions (or other the like, used by Christ or His apostle upon this occasion): –*

'According to the holy Institution, command, and example of our Blessed Saviour Jesus Christ, I take this Bread, and, having given thanks, break it, and give it unto you.'

*There the Minister, who is also himself to communicate, is to break the Bread, and give it to the Communicants.*

'Take ye, eat ye; this is the body of Christ, which is broken for you: do this in remembrance of him.'

*In like manner the Minister is to take the Cup, and say, in these expressions (or other the like, used by Christ or the apostle upon the same occasion): –*

'According to the institution, command, and example of our Lord Jesus Christ, I take this Cup, and give it unto you.'

*Here he giveth it to the Communicants.*

'This cup is the New Testament in the blood of Christ, which
is shed for the remission of the sins of many: drink ye all of it.'
*After all have communicated, the Minister may, in a few words, put them in
mind*

'Of the grace of God, in Jesus Christ held forth in this Sacrament;
and exhort them to walk worthy of it.'

*The Minister is to give solemn Thanks to God,*

'For His rich mercy, and invaluable goodness, vouchsafed to them
in that Sacrament; and to entreat for pardon for the defects of the
whole service, and for the gracious assistance of His good Spirit,
whereby they may be enabled to walk in the strength of that grace, as
becometh those who have received so great pledges of salvation.'

*The Collection for the Poor is to be ordered that no part of the public worship
is thereby hindered.*

# 35

# Baxter: *The Reformation of the Liturgy* 1661

In March 1661 King Charles II commissioned twelve bishops and twelve Presbyterian divines to meet in the Savoy 'to advise upon and review' the Book of Common Prayer. The Bishops requested the Presbyterians to submit in writing all their objections to the Prayer Book and all the additional forms and alterations they desired.

They presented the former in the *Exceptions*: the latter was drawn up by Baxter alone in *The Reformation of the Liturgy* which came to be known as *The Savoy Liturgy*. This work, although completed in a fortnight, was the product of long study and was notable for its dignity and its use of scripture. Professor Ratcliff has described Baxter's conception of the Lord's Supper as 'nearer to the historic western tradition than the conception which Cranmer embodied in the Communion Service of the Prayer Book of 1552' (*From Uniformity to Unity*, p. 123). The Liturgy met with no response from the bishops, however.

BIBLIOGRAPHY

Peter Hall, *Reliquiae Liturgicae: Documents connected with the Liturgy of the Church of England* (Bath 1847), vol. 4, pp. 9–33, 53–79.

W. Orme, *The Practical Works of the Revd Richard Baxter* (1830), vol. 15, pp. 450–527.

G. J. Cuming, *The Durham Book* (1961).

E. C. Ratcliff, (1) 'The Savoy Conference and the Revision of the Book of Common Prayer', in *From Uniformity to Unity 1662–1962*, edited by G. F. Nuttall and O. Chadwick (1962), pp. 89–148.

(2) 'Puritan Alternatives to the Prayer Book: *The Directory* and Richard Baxter's *Reformed Liturgy*' in *The English Prayer Book 1549–1662*, essays published for the Alcuin Club (1963), pp. 56–81.

# The Ordinary Public Worship on the Lord's Day

(This preceded the celebration of the Sacrament of the Body and Blood of Christ)

OPENING PRAYER FOR GOD'S ASSISTANCE (LONG AND SHORT FORMS)

APOSTLES' OR NICENE CREED, 'AND SOMETIMES ATHANASIUS' CREED'

TEN COMMANDMENTS

SCRIPTURE SENTENCES MOVING THE PEOPLE TO PENITENCE AND CONFESSION (OPTIONAL)

CONFESSION OF SIN AND PRAYER FOR PARDON AND SANCTIFICA-TION (LONG AND SHORT FORMS) ENDING WITH THE LORD'S PRAYER

SCRIPTURE SENTENCES 'FOR THE STRENGTHENING OF FAITH' (OPTIONAL)

PSALM 95 OR 100 OR 84

PSALMS IN ORDER FOR THE DAY

OLD TESTAMENT LESSON

PSALM OR TE DEUM

NEW TESTAMENT LESSON

PRAYER FOR THE KING AND MAGISTRATES

PSALM 67 OR 98 OR SOME OTHER, OR BENEDICTUS, OR MAGNIFICAT

PRAYER FOR THE CHURCH (EXTEMPORE)

SERMON

PRAYERS FOR A BLESSING ON THE WORD OF INSTRUCTION AND INTERCESSIONS

BENEDICTION (OMITTED WHEN THE SACRAMENT FOLLOWED)

# The Order of Celebrating the Sacrament
## Of the Body and Blood of Christ

EXHORTATION ON THE NATURE, USE AND BENEFITS OF THE
    SACRAMENTS (OPTIONAL)

EXHORTATION TO PENITENCE

PRAYER OF PENITENCE AND CONFESSION (BY THE MINISTER)

*Here let the Bread be brought to the Minister, and received by him, – and set upon the Table; and then let the Wine in like manner: or if they be set there before, however let him bless them, praying in these or the like words.*

Almighty God, thou art the Creator and the Lord of all things. Thou art the Sovereign Majesty whom we have offended. Thou art our most loving and merciful Father, who hast given thy Son to reconcile us to thyself: who hath ratified the new testament and covenant of grace with his most precious blood; and hath instituted this holy Sacrament to be celebrated in remembrance of him till his coming. Sanctify these thy creatures of bread and wine, which, according to thy institution and command, we set apart to this holy use, that they may be sacramentally the body and blood of thy Son Jesus Christ. Amen.

*Then (or immediately before this Prayer) let the Minister read the words of the institution, saying:*

Hear what the apostle Paul saith: For I have received of the Lord that which also I deliver unto you; that the Lord Jesus the same night in which he was betrayed, took bread, and when he had given thanks, he brake it, and said, Take, eat, this is my body which is broken for you: this do in remembrance of me. After the same manner also he took the cup, when he had supped, saying, This cup is the new testament in my blood; this do ye, as oft as ye drink it in remembrance of me: for as often as ye eat this bread, and drink this cup, ye do shew the Lord's death till he come.

*Then let the Minister say:*

This bread and wine, being set apart, and consecrated to this holy use by God's appointment, are now no common bread and wine, but sacramentally the body and blood of Christ.

*Then let him thus pray:*

Most merciful Saviour, as thou hast loved us to the death, and suffered for our sins, the just for the unjust, and hast instituted this holy Sacrament to be used in remembrance of thee till thy coming; we beseech thee, by thine intercession with the Father, through the sacrifice of thy body and blood, give us the pardon of our sins, and thy quickening Spirit, without which the flesh will profit us nothing. Reconcile us to the Father: nourish us as thy members to everlasting life. *Amen.*

*Then let the Minister take the Bread, and break it in the sight of the people, saying:*

The body of Christ was broken for us, and offered once for all to sanctify us: behold the sacrificed Lamb of God that taketh away the sins of the world.

*In like manner let him take the Cup, and pour out the Wine in the sight of the congregation, saying:*

We were redeemed with the precious blood of Christ, as of a Lamb without blemish and without spot.

*Then let him thus pray:*

Most holy Spirit, proceeding from the Father and the Son: by whom Christ was conceived; by whom the prophets and apostles were inspired, and the ministers of Christ are qualified and called: that dwellest and workest in all the members of Christ, whom thou sanctifiest to the image and for the service of their Head, and comfortest them that they may shew forth his praise: illuminate us, that by faith we may see him that is here represented to us. Soften our hearts, and humble us for our sins. Sanctify and quicken us, that we may relish the spiritual food, and feed on it to our nourishment and growth and grace. Shed abroad the love of God upon our hearts, and draw them out in love to him. Fill us with thankfulness and holy joy, and with love to one another. Comfort us by witnessing that we are the children of God. Confirm us for new obedience. Be the earnest of our inheritance, and seal us up to everlasting life. *Amen.*

*Then let the Minister deliver the Bread, thus consecrated and broken to the Communicants, first taking and eating it himself as one of them, when he hath said:*

Take ye, eat ye; this is the body of Christ, which is broken for you. Do this, in remembrance of him.

*In like manner he shall deliver them the Cup, first drinking of it himself, when he hath said:*

This cup is the New Testament in Christ's blood [or Christ's blood of the New Testament], which is shed for you for the remission of sins. Drink ye all of it, in remembrance of him.

*Let it be left to the Minister's choice, whether he will consecrate the bread and wine together, and break the bread, and pour out the wine immediately; or whether he will consecrate and pour out the wine, when the communicants have eaten the bread. If he do the latter, he must use the foregoing prayers and expressions twice accordingly. And then it be left to his discretion, whether he will use any words at the breaking of the bread and pouring out the wine, or not. And if the Minister choose to pray but once at the consecration, commemoration, and delivery, let him pray as followeth, or to this sense.*

Almighty God thou art the Creator and the Lord of all. Thou art the Sovereign Majesty whom we have offended. Thou art our merciful Father, who hast given us thy Son to reconcile us to thyself; who hath ratified the New Testament and covenant of grace with his most precious blood, and hath instituted this holy Sacrament to be celebrated in memorial of him till his coming. Sanctify these thy creatures of bread and wine, which, according to thy will, we set apart to this holy use, that they may be sacramentally the body and blood of thy Son Jesus Christ. And, through his sacrifice and intercession, give us the pardon of all our sins, and be reconciled to us, and nourish us by the body and blood of Christ to everlasting life. And to that end, give us thy quickening Spirit to shew Christ to our believing souls, that is here represented to our senses. Let him soften our hearts, and humble us for our sins, and cause us to feed on Christ by faith. Let him shed abroad thy love upon our hearts, and draw them on in love to thee, and fill us with holy joy and thankfulness, and fervent love to one another. Let him comfort us by witnessing that we are thy children, and confirm us for new obedience, and be the earnest of our inheritance, and seal us up to life everlasting, through Jesus Christ, our Lord and Saviour. Amen.

*Let it be left to the Minister's discretion, whether to deliver the bread and wine to the people, at the table, only in general, each one taking it and applying it to themselves: or to deliver it in general to so many as are in each particular form; or to put it into every person's hand: as also at what season to take the contribution for the poor. And let none of the people be forced to sit, stand, or kneel, in the act of receiving, whose judgment is against it.*

**THANKSGIVING**
**EXHORTATION (OPTIONAL)**
**HYMN OR PSALM OF PRAISE**
**BLESSING**

# 36

## The Book of Common Prayer 1662

The Savoy Conference had available a number of documents to assist in the review of the Book of Common Prayer. On the one side there were the Presbyterian *Exceptions* and Baxter's *Reformation of the Liturgy*; while on the other there were the Scottish Liturgy of 1637 and *The Durham Book*, containing the proposals of Cosin, Wren and Sancroft. The changes finally made in the 1552 rite were small, but none the less significant.

- a. The title 'The Prayer of Consecration' was used.
- b. Manual acts accompanied the recitation of the Institution Narrative.
- c. 'Amen' was inserted after the Institution Narrative.
- d. The addition of the 1549 words of administration to those of 1552, first made in 1559, was retained.
- e. Provision for additional consecration was made by the recitation of the Institution Narrative over further supplies of bread and wine.
- f. The consecrated elements remaining after communion were to be veiled until they were consumed at the end of the service.

BIBLIOGRAPHY

E. C. Ratcliff, *The Booke of Common Prayer: its Making and Revisions 1549–1661* (Alcuin Club Collections No. 37, 1949).

F. E. Brightman, *The English Rite*, (1915), 2 vols.

Cuming, pp. 145–67.

G. J. Cuming, *The Durham Book* (1961).
    'The Making of the Prayer Book of 1662' in *The English Prayer Book 1549–1662*, essays published for the Alcuin Club (1963), pp. 82–110.

W. J. Grisbrooke, *Anglican Liturgies of the Seventeenth and Eighteenth Centuries* (Alcuin Club Collections No. 40, 1958), pp. 349–74.

INTRODUCTORY RUBRICS
LORD'S PRAYER (PRIEST)
COLLECT FOR PURITY (PRIEST)

TEN COMMANDMENTS
COLLECT FOR THE KING
COLLECT OF THE DAY
EPISTLE
GOSPEL
NICENE CREED
NOTICES
SERMON OR HOMILY
OFFERTORY WITH SENTENCES
PRAYER FOR THE CHURCH MILITANT
EXHORTATIONS
INVITATION 'YE THAT DO TRULY . . .'
CONFESSION 'ALMIGHTY GOD, FATHER OF OUR LORD . . .'
ABSOLUTION 'ALMIGHTY GOD, OUR HEAVENLY FATHER . . .'
COMFORTABLE WORDS

*After which the Priest shall proceed, saying:*
           Lift up your hearts.
*Answer:*   We lift them up unto the Lord.
*Priest:*   Let us give thanks unto our Lord God.
*Answer:*   It is meet and right so to do.
*Then shall the Priest turn to the Lord's Table, and say:*
    It is very meet, right, and our bounden duty, that we should at all times and in all places, give thanks unto thee, O Lord, Holy Father, Almighty everlasting God.
*Here shall follow the proper Preface, according to the time, if there be any specially appointed: or else immediately shall follow:*
    Therefore with Angels and Archangels, and with all the company of heaven, we laud and magnify thy glorious Name, evermore praising thee, and saying, Holy, holy, holy, Lord God of Hosts, heaven and earth are full of thy Glory: Glory be to thee, O Lord most High. Amen.

PROPER PREFACES
*Upon Christmas Day, and seven days after.*
    Because thou didst give Jesus Christ . . .

*Upon Easter Day, and seven days after.*

  But chiefly are we bound to praise thee . . .

*Upon Ascension Day, and seven days after.*

  Through thy most dearly beloved Son Jesus Christ . . .

*Upon Whitsunday, and six days after.*

  Through Jesus Christ our Lord, according . . .

*Upon the Feast of Trinity only.*

  Who art one God, one Lord . . . (omitting 'holy Father')

*After each of which Prefaces shall immediately be sung or said,*

  Therefore with Angels and Archangels, and with all the company of heaven, we laud and magnify thy glorious Name, evermore praising thee, and saying, Holy, holy, holy, Lord God of hosts, heaven and earth are full of thy glory: Glory be to thee, O Lord most High. Amen.

*Then shall the Priest kneeling down at the Lord's Table, say in the name of all them that shall receive the Communion, this Prayer following.*

  We do not presume to come to this thy Table, O merciful Lord, trusting in our own righteousness, but in thy manifold and great mercies. We are not worthy so much as to gather up the crumbs under thy Table. But thou art the same Lord, whose property is always to have mercy: grant us therefore, gracious Lord, so to eat the flesh of thy dear Son Jesus Christ, and to drink his blood, that our sinful bodies may be made clean by his body, and our souls washed through his most precious blood, and that we may evermore dwell in him, and he in us. Amen.

*When the Priest, standing before the Table, hath so ordered the Bread and Wine, that he may with the more readiness and decency break the Bread before the people, and take the Cup into his hands, he shall say the Prayer of Consecration, as followeth:*

  Almighty God, our heavenly Father, who of thy tender mercy didst give thine only Son Jesus Christ to suffer death upon the Cross for our redemption; who made there (by his one oblation of himself once offered) a full, perfect, and sufficient sacrifice, oblation, and satisfaction, for the sins of the whole world; and did institute, and in his holy Gospel command us to continue, a perpetual memory of that his precious death, until his coming again; Hear us, O merciful Father, we most humbly beseech thee; and grant that we receiving these thy creatures of bread and wine, according to thy Son our Saviour Jesus Christ's holy institution, in remembrance of his death and passion, may be partakers of his most blessed Body and Blood: who in the same night that he was betrayed, [1]took Bread; and, when he had given thanks, [2]he brake it, and gave it to his disciples, saying, Take, eat; [3]this is my Body which is given for you: Do this in remembrance of me. Likewise after supper [4]he took the Cup; and, when he had given thanks, he gave it to them, saying, Drink ye all of this; for this[5] is my Blood of the New Testament, which is shed for you and for many for the remission of sins: Do this, as oft as ye shall drink it, in remembrance of me. *Amen.*

*Then shall the Minister first receive the Communion in both kinds himself, and then proceed to deliver the same to the Bishops, Priests, and Deacons, in like manner (if any be present), and after that to the people also in order, into their hands, all meekly kneeling. And, when he delivereth the Bread to any one, he shall say,*

The Body of our Lord Jesus Christ, which was given for thee, preserve thy body and soul unto everlasting life: Take and eat this in remembrance that Christ died for thee, and feed on him in thy heart by faith with thanksgiving.

*And the Minister that delivereth the Cup to any one shall say.*

The Blood of our Lord Jesus Christ, which was shed for thee, preserve thy body and soul unto everlasting life: Drink this in remembrance that Christ's blood was shed for thee, and be thankful.

*If the consecrated Bread or Wine be all spent before all have communicated, the Priest is to consecrate more, according to the Form before prescribed: Beginning at* [Our Saviour Christ in the same night, etc.] *for the blessing of the Bread; and at* [Likewise after Supper, etc.] *for the blessing of the Cup.*

*When all have communicated, the Minister shall return to the Lord's*

1. *Here the Priest is to take the paten into his hands:*
2. *And here to break the Bread:*
3. *And here to lay his hands upon all the Bread:*
4. *Here he is to take the Cup into his hand:*
5. *And here to lay his hand upon every vessel (be it Chalice or Flagon) in which there is any Wine to be consecrated.*

*Table, and reverently place upon it what remaineth of the consecrated Elements, covering the same with a fair linen cloth.*

LORD'S PRAYER
PRAYER OF OBLATION, 'O LORD OUR HEAVENLY FATHER, WE THY
    HUMBLE SERVANTS . . .'

*or* PRAYER OF THANKSGIVING
GLORIA IN EXCELSIS
BLESSING
FINAL RUBRICS AND COLLECTS